Da4

THE BATTLE OF HASTINGS

The

BATTLE

of

HASTINGS

THE FALL OF ANGLO-SAXON ENGLAND

Harriet Harvey Wood

Atlantic Books
LONDON

First published in hardback in Great Britain in 2008 by
Atlantic Books, an imprint of Grove Atlantic Ltd.

First published in paperback in Great Britain in 2009 by
Atlantic Books, an imprint of Grove Atlantic Ltd.

The picture acknowledgements on page 11 constitute an extension
of this copyright page.

1 3 5 7 9 8 6 4 2

A CIP catalogue record for this book is available from
the British Library.

978 1 84354 808 9

Design by Lindsay Nash

Printed in Great Britain

Atlantic Books
An imprint of Grove Atlantic Ltd
Ormond House
26–27 Boswell Street
London
WC1N 3JZ

www.atlantic-books.co.uk

To my sister

William the Bastard, having driven out the legitimate king of the English, seized the kingdom.

Annales Corbeienses

O fools and sinners! Why did they not ponder contritely in their hearts that they had conquered not by their own strength but by the will of almighty God, and had subdued a people that was greater, and more wealthy than they were, with a longer history: a people moreover amongst whom many saints and wise men and mighty kings had led illustrious lives, and won distinction in many ways at home and on the battlefield?

Orderic Vitalis, *Ecclesiastical History*, book IV

CONTENTS

LIST OF PLATES

Bayeux Tapestry (plate 1): Earl Harold talks with King Edward
© Bayeux/Giraudon/The Bridgeman Art Library
Bayeux Tapestry (plate 26): 'Where Harold makes his oath to Duke
William' © Bayeux/Giraudon/The Bridgeman Art Library
Jumièges Abbey Church courtesy of Nicholas J. Higham
Bayeux Tapestry (plate 28): '[Harold] comes to Edward' © Bayeux/
Giraudon/The Bridgeman Art Library
Hinged clasp from the Sutton Hoo burial mound © The Trustees
of the British Museum
Bayeux Tapestry (plate 31): 'Here sits Harold, King of the English'
© Bayeux/Giraudon/The Bridgeman Art Library
Harold's coinage © National Portrait Gallery, London
Bayeux Tapestry (plate 71): 'Here King Harold is killed' © Bayeux/
Giraudon/The Bridgeman Art Library
Bayeux Tapestry (plate 72): 'And the English turn in flight'
© Bayeux/Giraudon/The Bridgeman Art Library
Map of the battlefield drawn by General E. Renouard James
The Benedictional of St Æthelwold © British Library Images
Online

INTRODUCTION

Very few battles change history. The claim has been made for the battle of Waterloo, but Waterloo merely confirmed the course of a history that was clearly visible before it, but had been rudely interrupted by Napoleon's re-entry on the European stage. It marked a turning-point; it was not a catalyst. The battle of Britain is, perhaps, a stronger contender. Or the battle of Lepanto. William Golding has, with some justice, claimed the distinction for Thermopylae, on the grounds that it won thirty years' respite, enabling Athens to develop from a small provincial town to the city of Pericles that was to dominate the Mediterranean for centuries. 'If you were a Persian,' he writes, 'you could not know that this example would lead, next year, to the defeat and destruction of your whole army at the battle of Plataea, where the cities of Greece fought side by side. Neither you nor Leonidas nor anyone else could foresee that here thirty years' time was won for shining Athens and all Greece and all humanity.'[i]

Such a claim, if substantiated, means that what Leonidas and his Spartans achieved at Thermopylae ranks that desperate defence higher in its cultural implications than almost any other battle in history. John Stuart Mill claimed a similar distinction for the battle of Marathon, adding that it was more significant than the battle of

Hastings, even as an event in *English* history, since it changed the whole basis of western civilization. It is perhaps impossible to make a comparable claim for the significance of the battle of Hastings but it cannot be denied that it too was a battle that was to change the face of Europe, and cause a fundamental realignment between its major players. It was, wrote one eminent historian of the Anglo-Saxon period, one of the rare battles that have decided the fate of nations. Crécy, Agincourt, Magna Carta and much more lay implicit in the early-morning mist that hung over Caldbec Hill on 14 October 1066. But whatever the consequences of the battle, one fact is undisputed: it wiped out overnight a civilisation that, for its wealth, its political arrangements, its arts, its literature and its longevity, was unique in Dark Age Europe, and deserves celebration. In the general instability, lawlessness and savagery of the times, Anglo-Saxon England stood out as a beacon. Yet the timing of the battle and its result were the consequences of a series of accidents that could not have been predicted by either of the commanders. William, when he fought it, was generally known throughout Europe as William the Bastard. It has been suggested that he might more accurately have been known as William the lucky bastard.

Its outcome was far from a foregone conclusion. Any bookie, invited to give odds on the result a month before, would not have rated William's chances very high. The betting must always be against the invader of a country, especially when the invasion has to be by sea, and the defender is prepared for it. Had the winds been favourable and William been able to launch his attack even a month earlier, as he had hoped to do, it is highly likely that he would have been repelled with ignominy. Philip of Spain's later attempt at an invasion of England failed because the winds blew, and his great Armada was scattered. The English lost the battle of Hastings not least because the winds did not blow in the right direction at the right time.

It was a battle that was much more fully documented – in itself, in its causes and in its consequences – than almost any other battle that took place in western Europe in the Dark Ages. It is notable that, even at the time, it was recognized as an event of enormous historical significance. There is no shortage of testimony as to the events that led up to it nor to the conduct of the battle. The problem is that – with one exception – all this body of testimony comes from the winning side. The only contemporary English account, in the Anglo-Saxon Chronicle, is stark in its simplicity:

> Then came William Earl of Normandy into Pevensey on the eve of St Michael's mass, and as soon as he had disembarked his army, he built a castle at the port of Hastings. When this was told to King Harold, he gathered a great army and came against him at the hoar apple tree. And William came upon him unawares before his men were arrayed. But the king fought bravely against him with the men who would fight with him and there was much slaughter on either side. There were slain King Harold and Earl Leofwine his brother and Earl Gyrth his brother and many good men. And the Frenchmen held the place of slaughter. All as God granted it to them for the sins of the people.

On the Norman side there is, by contrast, almost a superfluity of accounts, both of the battle itself and of the events that led up to it. It will be important to establish (as far as possible) the status and interrelations of these, and a list of the most significant of them is provided in the Sources chapter. Ideally, it should be read before proceeding too far with the story, to understand the degree of authority of each. Through them it may be easier to see how it came about that King Harold lost a battle that it might have been thought impossible for him to lose and how the conquest and pillage of England took place under the banner and with the blessing of the Vicar of Christ.

This is a story that has often been told, and will go on being told as long as there are readers willing to read about it and writers to be drawn to its characters and events and to its insoluble puzzles and ambiguities. Almost all writers on the subject are partial on one side or the other and I am not less so than most. A recent eminent historian of the period has announced with his customary enthusiasm that, if he had been present, he would have been charging with William; I make no bones about stating that I would have stood beneath the standards of the Dragon of Wessex and the Fighting Man with Harold. For many years now the civilization of Anglo-Saxon England has seemed to me a wonderful and astonishing product of the late Dark Ages, a lamp to illuminate Europe, and its destruction at Hastings a matter for infinite regret. By 1066 it was an old civilization, and old civilizations tend to fall to energetic upstarts. With hindsight, and the advantages of modern research, it is possible to see how much of Anglo-Saxon England did actually survive the conquest, and that the combination of what survived with what was new produced a great deal that was equally worthwhile. But much also was lost.

THE BACKGROUND

The story that ended on the battlefield of Hastings began many years earlier, when the Danes resumed their invasions of England shortly after the accession to the English throne of Æthelred, known ignominiously but not entirely unjustifiably to history as the Unready. Viking raids had become familiar to the English in earlier years, and in a sense had never entirely ceased; but since their defeat by Alfred and his son, Edward the Elder, in the ninth and early tenth centuries and during the triumphant reign of Alfred's grandson, Athelstan, the Danes established in the north-east of England had gradually settled down into relatively law-abiding citizens. Athelstan's code of laws had made special provision for the punishment of crimes in their territory (which gradually came to be known – for obvious reasons – as the Danelaw) by Danish, rather than English, custom. Under Athelstan's immediate successors, such raids as there were seem to have been brief, uncoordinated affairs, designed to procure the maximum return in booty for the least investment in time and risk; during the reign of Edgar, remembered by later generations as a golden age of peace, they seem to have ceased completely. But Edgar died unexpectedly in 975, leaving two sons by successive wives, the elder, Edward, a teenager, and the younger, Æthelred, a child of ten. The character of Edward, despite his later sanctity as Edward the Martyr, appears to have been unattractive and to have boded ill for his future rule; none the less his assassination three years later by a faction supporting Æthelred was carried out in an act of treachery that appalled and sickened a society inured to almost every kind of violence. It would be too much to lay the blame for all that was to follow on the circumstances in which Æthelred began his reign; but there can be little doubt, judging from the contemporary chronicles, that they overshadowed it to an extent from which it never really recovered, and there can be equally little doubt that the temptation offered to the Danes by a wealthy kingdom ruled by a child of thirteen must have been irresistible.

It was not resisted. The first of the new generation of raiders arrived in 980, met only local opposition, ravaged Hampshire, Thanet and Cheshire and departed. More came in 981 and 982, and Devon was invaded in 988. The new Viking settlement of Normandy, established in 911 by a treaty between Charles the Simple of France and the Norwegian Hrolf Ganger (better known to history as Rollo), provided a convenient jumping-off point and refuge for these raiders, and the most notable response to their activities was a treaty in 991, brokered by the Pope, between Æthelred and Rollo's grandson, Duke Richard I of Normandy, which provided that neither should entertain the other's enemies. The treaty seems to have been more honoured in the breach than the observance, and it may have been in an attempt to secure a more effective understanding with Normandy that Æthelred in 1001 took as his second wife Emma, sister of Richard II of Normandy, a decision that was to prove fateful to England in future years. In the meantime, the raids continued and intensified. We would probably know little of one of the raids of Olaf Tryggvason, later King of Norway, had it not been the subject of one of the greatest late Old English poems, *The Battle of Maldon*. Olaf's herald announced the raiders' objectives to Byrhtnoth, the elderly ealdorman[ii] of Essex, in what must have been fairly standard terms:

> Bold seamen send me to you, and bid me say that you must speedily buy safety with treasure; far better is it for you to buy off this battle with tribute than that we should deal in bitter warfare. We need not destroy each other if you are generous to us; we are ready to establish peace for gold. If you, who are richest here, agree to ransom your people, and to give the seamen goods for truce in accordance with their demands and to accept peace from us, we will go back to our ships with the treasure, return to sea, and keep treaty with you.

Byrhtnoth rejects the raiders' demands scornfully ('Too shameful it seems to me that you should go with our treasure unopposed, now that you are come thus far into our land'). Although he held the causeway to the island where the invaders had landed, and could have defended it with not more than three men, he allows the Vikings to cross the Blackwater to the mainland so that they may fight on equal terms. Battle is joined, Byrhtnoth falls, some of his men desert, but his bodyguard fight around his corpse to the death, in accordance with the old Germanic tradition that held it shameful to survive a fallen leader. Many of the features of the battle of Maldon in 991 foreshadow with almost uncanny accuracy the later battle at Hastings.

Byrhtnoth's action may not have been as rash and quixotic as it seems in retrospect. If he had not allowed the Vikings to cross the causeway to fight, there was a risk that they might have taken to their ships and landed on a less well-defended part of the coast. It was his responsibility to hold them where there was at least an armed force in being to oppose them. If he had lived to give an account of his actions to the king, this might have been his excuse for his defeat. But in the story of the battle, as it has come down to us in the poem, the blame for the defeat is laid squarely on his chivalrous action – his *ofermod,* or overconfidence, as it is described in the text. In the immediate future, however, the most significant result of the battle of Maldon was that tribute was paid to the raiders within the next four months. How much was paid is not recorded; we do know that by a treaty later in the year 22,000 pounds of gold and silver was paid to Olaf Tryggvason for peace. When he returned in 994, it was in the company of Sweyn Forkbeard, son of Harold Bluetooth, King of Denmark, and with ninety-four warships. A further 16,000 pounds was paid. The next time the tribute amounted to 24,000 pounds. In 1002, in a political misjudgement that alone would have earned Æthelred the title of *Unræd* or 'Unready' (literally, 'no counsel', presumably a pun on the king's name, which means 'noble counsel', though there is no evidence that the nickname was used during his lifetime), he ordered the massacre of all the Danes in England on the grounds that he had heard that they were planning to assassinate him. The order was meaningless, because impossible to implement (in the Danelaw, there was virtually no one but Danes and the English with whom they had intermarried), but many were killed, among them Sweyn's sister Gunnhild who was in England as a hostage. To what extent this influenced Sweyn's later actions we do not know, but it can hardly have had an emollient effect. In 1003 and 1004 Sweyn, by this time King of Denmark, harried again in England. In 1007 he was paid 36,000 pounds. In 1009 he was back again with the most formidable army yet, and stayed. In 1012,

48,000 pounds was paid to them. The fact that these enormous sums could be raised comparatively quickly – by a tax that came to be known as the Danegeld – is testimony alike to the wealth of the country and to the efficiency of the fiscal system inherited by the king. By 1018, the total paid over since 991 came to a staggering 240,500 pounds, including a final payment of 18,500 pounds in 1018 to recompense the Danish army with which Cnut had conquered England. The figures are so vast that many historians have doubted whether they can be accurate, suggesting that they have been exaggerated by chroniclers. Recent research, however, has tended to vindicate the chroniclers.

The events of these disgraceful years are bitterly and sardonically recorded in the Anglo-Saxon Chronicle; in 1010 the chronicler writes,

> for three months they harried and burned, right into the wild fens. And they burned Thetford and Cambridge and then went southward to the Thames and those who were mounted rode towards the ships and then turned westward to Oxfordshire and thence to Buckinghamshire and so along the Ouse until they came to Bedford and so forth to Tempsford and burned everything wherever they went. Then they went to their ships with their plunder. And when they were dispersing to their ships, then our levies should have gone out again in case they decided to turn inland. Then the levies went home. And when the invaders were in the east, then our levies were in the west, and when they were in the south, then were our levies in the north. Then all the Witan [the king's Great Council] were called to the king to advise him how the land should be protected; but

whatever was advised lasted no longer than a month and
finally there was no man who would raise levies, but
each fled as far as he could. No shire would any longer
help its neighbour.

And all these misfortunes, he adds, befell the English through
lack of good counsel, in that tribute was not paid in time, but only
after the Danes had done as much harm as they could; 'and when
peace had been made and tribute paid, they went wherever they
would and raped and slew our wretched people'. The whole
country suffered from a collective loss of morale; Sweyn was
accepted as King of England in 1013, and at Christmas King
Æthelred followed his wife and his two sons by her into exile in
Normandy. He was to return to England and his throne for a brief
period after the death of Sweyn in February 1014, on condition
that he would rule better than he had done before (an interestingly
early constitutional agreement between people and king), and
died in London in 1016, leaving his eldest surviving son by his
first marriage, King Edmund Ironside, to defend England against
Sweyn's son Cnut. This he did effectively, winning four outright
victories before he was betrayed at the battle of Assandun later
in the same year. The struggle between Edmund and Cnut ended
in a peace treaty and the division of the kingdom between them;
but the suspicious death (almost certainly murder) of Edmund in
November 1016 left the whole of England in Cnut's hands.

It has been said that Cnut fought as the son of Sweyn
Forkbeard, but ruled as the brother of Edmund Ironside. The
chronicler William of Malmesbury reports him as praying at the
latter's tomb at Glastonbury. In one charter of 1018, he includes
the words 'when I, King Cnut, succeeded to the kingdom after
King Edmund'. Whatever his feelings for his former enemy,

fraternal or otherwise, they did not prevent him from sending the two infant sons of Edmund Ironside out of the country, delivering them to the King of Sweden with, according to some accounts, a request that they should be killed. This the Swedish king apparently felt unable to do but passed the children on to hosts elsewhere. At some stage during their wanderings, one of them died, but the survivor, Edward the Atheling[iii], eventually reached the court of Hungary where he grew to manhood, prospered and married. Nor did Cnut hesitate to eliminate the remaining sons of Æthelred by his first marriage. In the meantime, he established his rule over England, and sought to make it more acceptable by sending for Emma, the Norman widow of King Æthelred, and marrying her. Since she was presumably still living in Normandy at this time (though she may have returned with Æthelred in 1014), it seems likely that her remarriage took place with the approval of her brother, the Duke of Normandy. By her, Cnut had one son, Harthacnut, and a daughter; by an earlier, probably handfast marriage[iv] to an Englishwoman, Ælfgifu of Northampton (with whom he must have continued his relationship since she later appears in the records as co-regent in Norway), he already had two sons, Sweyn and Harold Harefoot, a situation that made future contention almost inevitable. In the short term, he was probably seeking to forestall any Norman attempt at the restoration of one of Emma's exiled sons by Æthelred by diverting the Duke of Normandy's attention from his nephews by Æthelred to his nephew by Cnut. In the meantime, he took over the administration of England very much as he inherited it from his predecessors: he recognized its ancient laws, honoured its Church and gave peace to a much-harassed people, largely through the fact that he was able to protect them from the Danish raids that in the recent past had played so large a part in disturbing it.

During the years that he ruled England, despite the bloodbath with which he began his reign, he achieved a greater degree of assimilation to and acceptance by the English than the later conqueror was to do. His brother, King Harald of Denmark, had died in 1018 or 1019, leaving Cnut to succeed to the Danish and, later, the Norwegian thrones in addition to the English. His dominions have been dubbed 'the Empire of the North'; the degree of his acceptance and security in England is best indicated by his ability to leave it to be governed by regents while he secured his position in Denmark and Norway.

What the extensive areas he controlled mainly did for England was to reopen to it the routes for trade and external contact, especially in the Baltic, from which it had been largely cut off during the troubles of Æthelred's reign. In this his personal choices and priorities made a substantial contribution to the peace and prosperity of England. Whatever his ability as a warrior (he is said to have declined Edmund Ironside's challenge to personal combat on the grounds that he was much the smaller), his diplomatic skills were clearly of a high order, and he welcomed the possibilities of interaction with the rulers of Europe. Sir Frank Stenton summarizes Cnut's achievements:

> His own conception of his place among sovereigns was
> expressed to all the world in 1027, when he travelled to
> Rome in order to attend the coronation of Conrad, the
> Holy Roman Emperor. In part, his journey was a work
> of devotion. Rome, to him, was the city of the apostles
> Peter and Paul, and its bishop was the teacher of kings.
> Early in his own reign he had received a letter from
> Pope Benedict VIII, exhorting him to suppress injustice,
> and to use his strength in the service of peace. In the

churches which he visited on the way to Rome he appeared as a penitent. But he was also a statesman, and there is no doubt that he regarded the coronation of an emperor as an appropriate moment for a gesture of respect towards the formidable power which threatened his Jutish frontier. It was also an opportunity for negotiations on behalf of traders and pilgrims from northern lands who had long been aggrieved by the heavy tolls levied at innumerable points on the road to Rome. Before the company dispersed he had secured valuable concessions from the emperor himself, the king of Burgundy, and the other princes through whose territory the great road ran. From the pope he obtained a relaxation of the immoderate charges hitherto imposed on English bishops visiting Rome for their *pallia*.[v]

The possibility that he may have aimed to model his rule on that of Alfred suggests itself. Alfred also made pilgrimages to Rome, Alfred also seized the opportunity while he was there to negotiate better terms and conditions for English pilgrims, Alfred also conducted international diplomacy on a scale of which few of his predecessors except Offa of Mercia were capable; and Alfred married his daughter into a European royal family, as Cnut was also later to do.

One minor innovation in particular was to establish itself in England. Cnut, as a king who had come to his throne by conquest rather than by rightful succession or election, perhaps understandably surrounded himself with a bodyguard of formidably efficient professional fighting men who became known as housecarls. Such a force may have been an innovation in England but in Denmark one had probably existed for some time. Cnut's grandfather, Harold Bluetooth, is said to have established a colony of such men at Jómsborg, at the mouth of the Oder. This was no casual Viking settlement but a body of men bound together by loyalty to the king and to each other and by a code of behaviour designed to promote the wellbeing and honour of the company. Several of the Danish housecarls had appeared in England during Æthelred's reign and played an active part in affairs during his successor's. Cnut's English bodyguard may have been constructed on the same lines as the Jómsborg Vikings (though there is no reference to such a body in his code of laws) and it gradually came to form the core of the English army, paid for by the Danegeld, more properly known as the heregeld or army tax; in many cases individual housecarls were rewarded with land, and the distinction between them and other of the king's thegns and landowners became imperceptible. The chief duty of the royal housecarls was to guard the king and to provide the first defence of the country in time of war. As time went on, the great lords of Anglo-Saxon England would have employed their own housecarls who would go to war with them; they became the eleventh-century equivalent of the *comitatus*, the body of retainers described by Tacitus in his *Germania,* who served their lord in war and defended him to the death. The army that fought at Hastings would have included both royal housecarls and those of the chief landowners who were present at the battle.

The strongest recommendation of Cnut's reign, as has been remarked, is that his contemporaries found so little to say about it. His comparatively early death in 1035 left the kingdom to the chaos of a disputed inheritance. Neither he nor any of his sons appears to have been physically robust. It is an ironic reflection that, if Cnut had been as healthy and lived as long as Edward the Confessor (there cannot have been more than a few years between them in age), there would never have been a Norman Conquest. It is probable that Cnut had intended his son by Emma to succeed him; but Harthacnut's absence in Denmark at the time of his father's death left the way open for his half-brother, Harold Harefoot (Sweyn had predeceased his father), to fill the vacancy, first theoretically as regent until Harthacnut could return, but later as King Harold I. His tenure of the throne was brief; but it included one event that was to produce reverberations as late as 1066.

During Cnut's relatively peaceful reign, his stepsons Edward and Alfred, Emma's children by Æthelred, had grown up in Normandy. We know little of their life there. They do not seem, for example, ever to have been granted land or honours in Normandy when they reached adulthood, though their sister was respectably married to the Count of the Vexin. On the occasions when they appear as charter witnesses there, their names generally occur rather insultingly low in the order of precedence. In 1033 William's father, Duke Robert, assembled a fleet for the purpose, it was said, of assisting the young athelings to regain their inheritance. The fleet lay for some time at Jersey and then sailed for Mont St Michel to attack Brittany instead. It was hardly a convincing gesture of support. On the other hand, they do appear to have been recognized as the rightful heirs of their father, despite their mother's subsequent marriage to his conqueror and the birth of another son. Emma herself appears to have remembered them only intermittently, at least in public, her main ambitions being centred on her son Harthacnut, a fact that aroused the lasting resentment of her eldest son Edward. In 1036 the younger brother, Alfred the Atheling, returned to England, to visit his mother at Winchester. According to the anonymous author of the life of Emma, he was lured over by a forged letter from Harold Harefoot, written in Emma's name, asking that one of her sons come to her immediately to discuss how the throne might be regained.[vi] Whether this story is true or not, it is unlikely that he was coming simply to make a social call. On the other hand, he does not seem to have arrived in any kind of strength. According to the life of Emma, he brought only a few men. He was intercepted by Godwin, Earl of Wessex and handed over by him to King Harold Harefoot who had Alfred's men murdered or mutilated and the Atheling himself blinded so savagely that he died of his wounds at Ely.

Blinding was not at that time a very unusual punishment (after 1066 it was, for example, the penalty for poaching one of the royal deer). Like other forms of mutilation common at the time (and promoted by the Church in England as a more merciful fate than death), it was designed to render the victim harmless. None the less in this instance it created consternation. (It may be noted that it is unlikely that so common an act of Dark Age violence would have aroused such surprise or revulsion in other countries; that it did so in England indicates the extent to which a less savage and more law-abiding society had prevailed there.) Harold Harefoot's motives are perfectly clear; the Atheling posed an obvious threat to his power. Godwin's motives are less clear. He had voted for Harthacnut's succession and against Harold after Cnut's death, and this may have appeared a way to reinstate himself in the king's good graces. In later years, when he came to trial for his part in the crime, he maintained that in surrendering Alfred to Harold's men, he was acting under the king's orders and had not known that the Atheling's mutilation was intended. Whatever the facts of the case, it shocked the inhabitants of England, most of whom had probably virtually forgotten the Atheling's existence during the peaceful days of Cnut's reign. Never was a bloodier deed done in this land since the Danes came, declared the Anglo-Saxon

Chronicle, which recorded the death of 'the guiltless Atheling' in a burst of poetry. Whatever Godwin's motives, his part in the crime permanently stained his name and soured his relations with Alfred's brother Edward when the latter eventually succeeded to the throne. Not the least of the Norman accusations against Godwin's son Harold in future years would be the fact that his father had betrayed a prince of the royal house of Wessex who was kin to their duke and was under Norman protection.

If Godwin had hoped to propitiate Harold Harefoot by his betrayal of the Atheling, he might have saved himself the trouble. Within four years Harold was dead, succeeded by his half-brother, Harthacnut, who had been Godwin's candidate for the throne all along. Harthacnut lasted a bare two years on the throne before dropping dead at a bridal feast, but during his short reign he invited his half-brother, the Atheling Edward, by now the only surviving son of Æthelred, to return to England and (it is assumed) to succeed him. Thus, after a gap of twenty-four years, the direct heir of the royal house of Wessex returned to the English throne.

It is difficult, on the limited evidence available, to assess the character of King Edward fairly. In part, this is due to the atmosphere of piety spread retrospectively over his life by the appellation – which he acquired only after his death – of St Edward the Confessor. What is definitively known of him suggests that his later sainthood may have been no more deserved than the title of 'the Martyr' was merited by his uncle Edward, assassinated in 978 for the benefit of his father Æthelred. The only thing we know of his personality is that he seems to have had a tendency to fly into ungovernable rages. The main characteristic that can be deduced from his policies is a determination never to leave England again. The situation in England to which he returned, though clearly preferable to his former position of impoverished hanger-on at the ducal court in Normandy, cannot have been without difficulty, and it is much to his credit that he negotiated it so successfully that he contrived (though clearly no warrior-king, like his half-brother Edmund Ironside) to die peacefully in his bed after a relatively prosperous reign of twenty-four years. His biography, the *Vita Ædwardi Regis,* commissioned by his wife, portrays him as an old man, majestic, white-haired and white-bearded, all his thoughts fixed on the next world. He is probably more realistically described by his twentieth-century biographer:

> If there is one trait that runs through the whole and can usefully be stressed at the beginning, it is Edward's ability to survive. Despite an inclination to rashness and inflexibility, he was blessed with a saving caution. And there is a general characteristic which must be held in mind. Edward was never a *roi fainéant* or a puppet ruler. Although he was neither a wise statesman nor a convincing soldier, he was both belligerent and worldly-wise. He caused most of his enemies to disappear and outlived almost all who had disputed his authority. He was *rex piissimus,* a fortunate king, blessed by Heaven.[vii]

Since, however, it was during his reign that the faultlines that were to lead to Hastings became perceptible, we must make some effort to understand him.

He was born in or around 1005, and can therefore have been a child of no more than seven or eight when his mother took him to her native Normandy as an exile. He seems to have made a brief reappearance in England when his father Æthelred was restored to his throne in 1014. Apart from one or two rather half-hearted skirmishes around the coast, he saw no more of England until his return as heir-presumptive to Harthacnut in 1041. Since he was educated from childhood at the Norman court, we may assume that he was bred to arms as no other form of education for a king's son would have been contemplated there. Whatever his belligerent impulses, he seems never to have put such an education into practical use. There is no credible evidence of his appearance on any battlefield. According to the Scandinavian *Flateyjarbók*, he fought beside his brother Edmund in 1016 and nearly killed Cnut, but this is a very late fourteenth-century source and cannot be regarded as reliable. Since he could only have been eleven or twelve at the time, this story seems particularly unlikely. Cnut may not have been a great warrior, making up in guile what he lacked in physical prowess, but he cannot have been as feeble as that. Of the personalities who then dominated England he knew nothing. It is improbable that he even spoke much English. If he did, it would certainly have been as a foreigner. In the first few years after his return, he must have had much to learn. One of the things he must have learned very quickly was that, though he enjoyed a substantial reservoir of goodwill in the country as a whole as the last representative of the line of Alfred, in practice he held the throne only through the continuing support of the dominant nobles of the kingdom, and in particular three of them: Siward, Earl of Northumbria; Leofric, Earl of Mercia; and Godwin, Earl of Wessex. All three had originally been appointed by Cnut; all enjoyed considerable power in their own domains. The prospect of asserting his authority over them might well have daunted more forceful men than Edward.

His first conspicuous action, almost as soon as he was crowned, was with the support of all three and revealed much both about Edward's own character and the reserves of resentment he felt he had to pay off. In company with the three great earls, he rode without warning to Winchester where his mother, Emma, was living, stripped her of all that she owned, 'untold riches in silver and gold', and abandoned her there with a bare subsistence. The reason given for this in one version of the Anglo-Saxon Chronicle is that in past days she had been very hard towards him, and had done less for him than he had wished before he was king. A more practical reason may have been that she had control of the royal treasury, which was normally kept in Winchester, the old capital of the kingdom. She may have been holding it on behalf of her son Harthacnut, and using it to interfere in matters of state (one version of the Chronicle states that she was holding it 'against him'). The fact that he was accompanied on his raid by the three most powerful men in the land indicates that there was more than a private grudge here, but a private grudge there must undoubtedly have been, and the fact that it, rather than a perfectly legitimate public reason, is officially recorded in the Chronicle suggests that it must have been widely known. Whatever lay behind his actions, it signalled Emma's retirement from public life. Her death is recorded in 1051.

In the meantime, Edward had to come to terms with the main men of his new kingdom. Of the three great earls, his most difficult relationship was with Godwin. To begin with, Godwin was on his doorstep. Northumbria was far distant, alien, Danish territory, and Edward would not be the first King of England never to visit it. There is no evidence that his father ever went there, apart from an attack on the Danes in Cumbria in 1000. Siward, a Dane himself, was powerful, but he concerned himself only minimally with the affairs of central government; his chief preoccupations were with his frontier with Scotland and with potential threats from Scandinavia. Mercia, stretching right across the English midlands from Wales to the North Sea, was nearer, but not near enough to demand Edward's attention on a daily basis; and with Leofric he had no quarrel. Wessex, which included most of the south of England, including London, Winchester and most of the king's own lands, was unavoidable, and with Godwin he had a very definite quarrel, since he held him responsible for the death of his younger brother Alfred. On the other hand, Godwin seems to have played the greatest part in supporting Edward's claim to the throne. This was almost certainly not entirely disinterested. Godwin had six sons who needed to be provided with earldoms, and he had daughters, one of whom might prove to be the mother of an heir to the throne. We do not know what arguments were used to persuade Edward that Godwin's eldest daughter, Edith, would make him a suitable queen. Whatever they were, he did not resist them, and the marriage took place in 1044. To Edith herself, there seem to have been no objections; records describe her as beautiful, accomplished, well-educated and pious. From surviving stories, she also appears to have been humourless, acquisitive and arrogant. None the less, marriage to the daughter of the man whom Edward regarded as responsible for his brother's death must have been an unwelcome pill to swallow, and the fact that the marriage proved childless raised inevitable speculation.

At the outset of Edward's reign, the lack of an obvious heir cannot have appeared as a serious problem to anyone. Aged no more than thirty-eight when he succeeded to the throne, he had ample time to provide an heir of his own body, and his wife, who must have been in her early twenties when she married, came of a conspicuously prolific family. The legend of Edward's vow of lifelong celibacy had its origins later in his reign, and, in due course, did much to strengthen his claims to sanctity; but it is not impossible that, jostled into marriage with the daughter of the man against whom he maintained an unremitting grudge, he hit on this expedient to deny Godwin what he wanted most: a grandson who was heir to the throne. It would have been typical of what can be deduced of his sense of humour.

It was only in 1051 that the cracks in the political façade began to surface. They showed then through an incident that seemed, in its apparent total irrelevance and irrationality, entirely unplanned. Edward's brother-in-law, Eustace of Boulogne, second husband of his sister Godgifu, came to England on a visit to the king at Gloucester, and, in the words of one version of the Anglo-Saxon Chronicle, 'spoke with him what he would' and set off home. As he approached Dover, he and his men stopped to eat, and, for no explained reason, put on their armour. In Dover, they attempted to commandeer lodgings by force. One of Eustace's men wounded a householder when he tried to enter his home against his will and was killed by the outraged townsman. A riot immediately broke out; Eustace and his men slew the townsman on his own hearth and then more than twenty other men throughout the town. The citizens retaliated by killing nineteen of Eustace's men and wounding as many more. Eustace escaped with his remaining followers and returned to the king at Gloucester where he appears to have given Edward a very one-sided account of the fracas. The king, enraged, sent for Godwin and ordered him to carry war into Dover and punish the town. Godwin refused, being loath, as the Chronicle reports, to harm his own people.

The reports of the incident raise many questions, few of which can be pursued in detail here. Why did Eustace come to talk to his brother-in-law at this particular time? Boulogne was a long-standing ally of England, there might have been good diplomatic reasons for Eustace's visit, but they are not explained in the sources. Why did Eustace, on his journey home, stop to arm before entering Dover? There was no reason why the townspeople should have been assumed to be hostile until they were provoked. Whatever lay behind it, the consequences were great. Godwin's refusal to punish the town infuriated the king, who summoned the most important men in the country to Gloucester for a meeting of the Witan, the general council of the kingdom. The coincidence with these events of a rising by the Welsh on the frontier in the earldom of Godwin's eldest son Sweyn may have been chance or may not. Accusations against Godwin, who had become too powerful too fast, were being made to the king. Robert of Jumièges, the Norman Archbishop of Canterbury (who had managed to insinuate himself into the appointment against Godwin's candidate, though the latter was supported by the monks of Canterbury), alleged that Godwin was plotting Edward's death as he had plotted his brother's. In the meantime, Godwin with his sons Sweyn and Harold were assembling their men at Beverstone in order to go to the king in force to present their case. The northern earls Siward and Leofric, summoned to a meeting of the Witan, arrived with a modest entourage but, finding the south in uproar, sent hastily for reinforcements to support the king. There was then a period of stand-off. The forces confronting each other must have been fairly evenly balanced, but it is noticeable that no one was prepared to strike the first blow or be responsible for tipping the country into civil war. It was realized, says the Chronicle, that this would be great unwisdom, since it would leave the kingdom open to attack by its enemies. This is worth marking as possibly the first recorded instance of all the great men of the kingdom deliberately drawing back from war in the interests of the country at large. The matter was adjourned to a hearing in London in September, to which Godwin and his sons were summoned to defend themselves against accusations of treason.

By the time of the hearing, Edward had, with considerable adroitness, strengthened his position to such an extent that he was able to order Godwin to present himself in court with no more than twelve men to support him; he refused, through Stigand, Bishop of Winchester, to give Godwin hostages for his safety, adding the slightly sinister message that Godwin could have peace and pardon only when he returned to Edward his brother Alfred, alive and well, with all his followers and possessions. Godwin, a pragmatic man if ever there was one, rode to the coast and took ship for Flanders with all his family, except his sons Harold and Leofwine who fled to the Viking kingdom of Dublin. Edward sent Bishop Ealdred in pursuit of Harold and Leofwine, but he could not catch them, 'or [said the Chronicle] he would not'. All were outlawed. Queen Edith was stripped of her possessions and consigned to the custody of the king's half-sister, who was Abbess of Wherwell. There are indications that considerable pressure was put on Edward to divorce her, probably by Robert of Jumièges. If there was, he resisted it. It was a wonderful business, says the Chronicle, because Godwin was so exalted that he ruled the king and all England, and his sons were earls and the king's favourites.

Flanders was a natural refuge for English political exiles. Together with Normandy, it had also proved, over the past century, a convenient jumping-off point for Viking marauders, and an equally convenient place for them to sell the booty they obtained in England. Much of Edward's foreign policy was designed to neutralize or contain the hostility of the Count of Flanders; the recent marriage of Godwin's third son, Tostig, to the count's half-sister can have done as little to reassure Edward as the marriage of William of Normandy to the count's daughter Matilda at about this time. There were suspicions that William's choice of Matilda could have been influenced by the fact that she could claim descent from King Alfred through her father. Godwin lay low and waited.

In the meantime, the D Chronicle, the northern version, records an event unnoted by any other sources, English or Norman. Immediately after the outlawing of the Godwin family, it says, Earl William came from beyond the sea with many Frenchmen and was received by the king and then went home again. If William of Normandy did indeed pay a visit to Edward at this time, it is almost incredible that this is not mentioned by the E or C versions of the Chronicle, especially E, which is so closely associated with Canterbury and whose writer must have been much nearer to the scene of action than the author of the D version. However, there are many instances throughout the history of the Chronicle when its silence in a certain year is contradicted by evidence in other sources that recordable events had in fact taken place. This may be one example of an inexplicable silence, and the absence of comment in E and C, therefore, cannot necessarily be taken to mean that William's visit did not happen. It is, however, even more incredible that it should not have been recorded by the Norman chroniclers, who could have turned it to so much advantage when William needed to bolster his claim to the throne. There are, as will be seen, good reasons for doubting whether the visit ever took place. But either way, there is plenty of evidence that in Godwin's absence foreigners, particularly Normans, were in the ascendent at court.

In the meantime Godwin was preparing to try his luck in England again. Harold and Leofwine made a preliminary raiding expedition from Dublin to Porlock in summer 1052 and then retreated after harrying Porlock and its environs and provisioning their ships. Godwin left the river Yser on 22 June and arrived off Sandwich, after landing briefly at Dungeness where he received a warm welcome. The king sent out ships to take him but Godwin evaded them and, when a storm blew up, returned to Bruges. The king, in a piece of strategy reminiscent of his father, then decommissioned part of his fleet to save money. A rendezvous between Godwin and his sons was eventually effected in August, and their united fleet sailed along the south coast of Sussex and Kent, carefully refraining from any kind of harrying or pressure of the inhabitants of what had been part of Godwin's earldom. They did, however, encourage volunteers, and by the time they rounded the North Foreland had assembled a formidable fleet and army, with which they sailed up the Thames as far as Southwark, where Godwin had a large manor and where the Londoners were generally friendly to him. The king had sent out an appeal for troops and ships but the response was slow. On this occasion, Godwin had the advantage in strength and was given passage through London Bridge by the townspeople. Once through, he drew up his ships to encircle the king's and the two fleets sat and looked at each other.

Godwin sent emissaries to the king to open negotiations, asserting that he had no desire to attack and only sought permission to come before the king and clear himself. Leofric and Siward made it equally clear that they were not prepared to fight Godwin. Civil war could only damage their lands and property, and they may, for all we know, have been as opposed to the idea of foreign domination at court as Godwin clearly was. Robert of Jumièges and his friends read the writing on the wall, as Godwin had done a year earlier. They did not wait for Godwin to meet the king but fled London, killing a number of the townspeople in their haste, sailed from Essex in a clapped-out old ship and made for Normandy; they left behind Robert's pallium, the symbol of his position as archbishop, in their hurry. Stigand, acting once again as intermediary, arranged the audience with the king, where Godwin and Harold, fully armed, threw themselves at his feet, casting aside their weapons, and asked for leave to clear themselves. Edward, in no position to refuse, listened to Godwin's case, gave him the kiss of peace and restored to him and his sons (with the exception of Sweyn, whose murder of his cousin Bjorn and abduction and rape of the abbess of Leominster had sent him on pilgrimage to Jerusalem in the course of which he died) the earldoms that had been forfeited. His short bid for independence from the Godwins was over. The queen returned from Wilton to which she seems to have been moved from Wherwell and resumed her usual place at the king's side. Stigand's diplomatic efforts were rewarded with Robert's archbishopric of Canterbury, which he continued to hold in plurality with his bishopric of Winchester; this caused great offence in Rome, not so much because Stigand retained Winchester (holding appointments in plurality was deplored but hardly unusual in the eleventh century), but because Robert had been uncanonically superseded. The offence was compounded by the fact that Stigand economically kept Robert's pallium for his own use.

The king did not have to maintain his appearance of friendship with Godwin for very long. Godwin died in 1053, felled by a stroke at the king's Easter feast. He was succeeded as Earl of Wessex by his son Harold who thus became the richest and most powerful man in the kingdom. On the death of Siward in 1055, Tostig, Harold's next brother, received his earldom of Northumbria; Mercia passed to Ælfgar, Leofric's son, on his father's death in 1057; and Gyrth, Godwin's fourth son, succeeded to East Anglia, which had been held successively by Harold and Ælfgar. The possessions of the Godwin family, added together, dwarfed the king's. On the other hand, Harold's relationship with the king was much easier than his father's had been, and it seems clear that Edward gradually came to rely on his strength and ability more and more, to the extent that he is described in the Chronicles as *subregulus,* under-king. Edward's relations with Tostig seem to have been even warmer. But there was still no heir, and it was clearly unlikely that Edward and Edith would have a child, still less that he would have reached an age to be able to rule by the time his father died. It may have been the urging of his councillors that persuaded Edward to look elsewhere for a successor, and remember that his half-brother, King Edmund Ironside, had left sons. One of them, Edward the Atheling or Exile, was still living at the court of Hungary, and steps were taken to fetch him home to England as heir-apparent.

There were diplomatic problems over this, caused by wars between Flanders, the German emperor and Hungary. Bishop Ealdred of Worcester was sent with a mission to Cologne in 1054 to seek the help of Emperor Henry III of Germany in contacting the King of Hungary and negotiating for the return of the Atheling. But the diplomatic relations between Germany and Hungary were strained at this time, and, after waiting for a year, Ealdred was obliged to come home without success. The death of Henry III in 1056 made it possible for a second attempt to be made, and it may well have been Earl Harold who made it; his name as witness to a Flemish diploma issued by his brother-in-law, the Count of Flanders on 13 November 1056 is suggestive. The count himself travelled on to Cologne and Regensberg where he spent Christmas; if Harold went with him, it would not have been difficult to contact the Hungarian court from Regensburg. There is no proof that he did so, other than an indication in the *Vita Ædwardi* that Harold had been travelling on the Continent at about this time, and the fact of his witnessing of the Flemish diploma. Whether through Harold's persuasions or not, the Atheling did agree to return, though it was not till 1057 that he reached English soil. He brought with him a Hungarian wife, Agatha, his son, Edgar, and two daughters, Margaret and Christina. Within days of landing in London, he died without even seeing his uncle, and was buried in St Paul's. It was inevitable that there should have been suspicions of foul play, but it is hard to see whom a murder could have benefited. Not the king, certainly, and not the chief men of the kingdom who were desperate for a clear, undoubted heir. If Harold had privately had his sights on the throne at this date (and there is no evidence that he had), it would have been a simple matter for him to prevent the exile's return or to have him murdered much further from England. Nor had there ever been suspicions of this kind against him, though there had been allegations of the kind against William of Normandy, several of whose opponents met deaths in doubtful circumstances. It is far more probable that the exile died from natural causes; he had undergone a long and dangerous journey, he was a middle-aged man of about forty (elderly by contemporary standards though no older than Harold was to be in 1066), and may well have been in poor health anyway. The Witan was left with his son, Edgar, a child of six.

THE CONTENDERS

The question of the succession to Edward is clouded by uncertainty and lack of conclusive evidence, but this has not prevented innumerable scholars from attempting to assess the legitimacy of the competition. In a sense, the question is irrelevant, since the problem was ultimately to be resolved by force, but the various possibilities are of some importance in accounting for the actions of the people involved. In the mid-eleventh century there was no right of primogeniture in England either for the throne or in family inheritance to the extent that there was in Normandy and some other parts of Europe. Kingship was elective, though with a prejudice in favour of candidates from the ruling house. The situation regarding kingship in England was set out concisely by the monk and homilist Ælfric at the end of the tenth century:

> No man can make himself king, but the people have the choice to elect whom they like; but after he is consecrated king, he has authority over the people, and they cannot shake his yoke off their necks.[viii]

The child Edgar was only one of many who saw themselves as rivals for England, though lineally he may have had the best claim. He was of the royal blood, throne-worthy. The title of 'atheling' was normally reserved for the sons of reigning kings, and Edward the Exile had never reigned. The fact, therefore, that he was known as the Atheling in King Edward's lifetime is significant and implies that Edward regarded him as a likely successor – which in itself undermines William's claim that the king had given his promise to him. Lineage, however, was only one of several factors to be considered before a new king of England was crowned. Descent from the royal line of Wessex was important; but it was far from being the most important requirement. The emphasis throughout the pre-conquest period seems to have been on the most credible candidate whenever there was a choice, as there usually was. The main consideration was the safety of the kingdom; in considering the claims of Edgar, the king's councillors would not have forgotten the invasions and ultimate conquest that had followed the child Æthelred's accession in 978. In the past a deceased king's eldest son might have been passed over, because he was too young, because it was not felt that he was the best man to defend the realm or because there was a later son by a more powerful mother. It was said that Emma had made it a condition of her marriage to Æthelred that their sons should take precedence over his sons by his previous marriage. In fact, Æthelred was succeeded by Edmund Ironside, a son of the earlier marriage, because Emma's sons were not of an age to oppose Cnut nor on the spot. Anglo-Saxon kings tended to die young, leaving eldest sons of tender years. King Alfred himself had succeeded three elder brothers who had held the throne in turn, one of whom (Æthelred I) had left at least one son, partly because it had been so set down in the will of his father, King Æthelwulf, but mainly because he was deemed the best available defender of the kingdom against the Danes at that time and his nephew was young and untried. If Alfred had not already proved himself a competent general, it is probable that his father's will would have been disregarded or at least challenged. Later, his own eldest son and successor had to deal with the resentment of the cousin who felt his claims had been set aside. However, Edgar, despite his youth, was still a factor, as was shown by his election as king by all the councillors in London, as soon as the death of Harold at Hastings was known.

The main considerations in the selection of the heir were royal blood; nomination by the late king; election by the Witan; and the ability to defend the kingdom. With the death of Edward the Exile, the king's councillors were left with no one who fulfilled all of them. Edgar, grandson of King Edmund Ironside, had the royal blood, but was not, by age, upbringing or experience, qualified to undertake the land's defence. There were the two sons of King Edward's own sister, Godgifu, who, like her brothers, had been brought up in Normandy and had been married, first to Count Drogo of the Vexin, and, after his death, to Count Eustace of Boulogne, the author of the fracas at Dover. Her elder son, Walter, had succeeded his father as Count of the Vexin, but had been offered the county of Maine in his wife's right on the death of her brother the Count of Maine in 1051; Walter and his wife died by what was reputed to be poison shortly after William of Normandy's conquest of Maine to which, he claimed, he had been promised the succession himself. The fact that Walter was so close in line to the English throne and that he and his wife were in Norman custody at the time they died did nothing to allay the suspicions that their deaths inevitably aroused. Orderic Vitalis says carefully that they were poisoned 'by the evil machinations of their enemies', of whom William was certainly one of the most prominent; he repeats the allegation later in his history. Poisoning was certainly not uncommon at the Norman court; William of Jumièges suggests that Duke Richard III was poisoned by his brother, William's father, Duke Robert. Walter's younger brother, Ralph, had followed his uncle Edward to England shortly after his succession and had been made Earl of Hereford; he was known in England, unenviably, as Ralph the Timid, and if he was of a naturally unwarlike disposition, the rule of an earldom on the Welsh marches can have done little to encourage him. He died in 1057, in the same year as Edward the Exile, leaving an infant son and was therefore out of the running, though in view of his reputation, it is unlikely that he would have received many votes in the Witan anyway.

Outside the king's close relatives, there were a number of other claimants. One of the most formidable, as well as the most absurd in lineal terms, was Harald Sigurdsson, King of Norway, known to history as Harald Hardrada or Harald Hardcounsel. His claim went back beyond King Edward to the reign of King Harthacnut who, he maintained, had made an agreement with Harald's nephew, King Magnus Olafson of Norway, before Harthacnut returned to England to claim his crown and while he was at war with Magnus for the crown of Denmark. By this agreement, whichever of the two of them should outlive the other would inherit the other's kingdom (or kingdoms, since Magnus continued to claim Denmark as well as England by right of this agreement); and under it, Harald maintained his claim to both the English and the Danish crowns as the heir and successor of King Magnus. Much of Harald Hardrada's time as King of Norway was absorbed by his struggle with King Sweyn Estrithson for the Danish crown; if he had chosen to enforce his English claim earlier, he would have been a formidable threat, for he was regarded as beyond doubt the strongest and most dreaded warrior of his age and had, during a long life of battle and plunder in most parts of Europe and Byzantium, earned a reputation for courage, guile, cruelty and greed second to none. In his youth, after the death of his half-brother, King Olaf (later St Olaf), at the battle of Stiklestad where he also fought, he had fled through Sweden and the Viking states in Russia to Byzantium where he joined, and very soon captained, the renowned Varangian Guard, the elite Scandinavian bodyguard of the emperor. The Varangians' reputation for expertise in every form of warfare was well deserved, and their skills were kept well honed by the continual wars, internal and external, that the Byzantine emperors were engaged in. They were also specialists in the acquisition of plunder, from which Harald is reputed to have amassed a colossal fortune. He left Byzantium in 1043, returned through Kiev, marrying Grand Prince Yaroslav's daughter Elisabeth on the way, and reached Sweden in 1045. His immediate goal was the throne of Norway, held then by his nephew, Magnus Olafsson; after much negotiation, bloodshed and chicanery he eventually achieved a joint kingship with Magnus, inheriting the whole kingdom when Magnus died childless in 1047. Harald was then free to continue his struggle with Sweyn Estrithson for the throne of Denmark. His designs on England were well known there.

Sweyn Estrithson, son of Cnut's sister Estrith, had his own claim to England to maintain. As Cnut's nephew – who had survived Cnut's sons – he was heir to a former King of England and he asserted that Edward the Confessor had promised that he should inherit if Edward died childless. There are reasons to doubt the likelihood of this promise. Sweyn was closely connected with the Godwin family. His father, Ulf, husband of Cnut's sister Estrith, was brother of Godwin's wife Gytha; Godwin had certainly fostered Sweyn's brother Bjorn in his family, and Bjorn had made his home in England and prospered there, until he was treacherously murdered by Godwin's eldest son, Sweyn. Sweyn Estrithson may also have spent part of his boyhood at least in the Godwin household. The idea that Edward would voluntarily bequeath his throne to Godwin's nephew by marriage, even though he was Cnut's heir in Denmark, is implausible. When Sweyn appealed to Edward in 1049 for ships to help him in his struggle with Magnus of Norway, and Godwin sensibly recommended sending them since Magnus was much stronger than Sweyn and was known to be planning an invasion of England, Edward refused to help (with, according to the D Chronicle, the support of all the people). On the other hand, Edward spent much of the early part of his reign under threat from Danish invasions, since Sweyn Estrithson had expected to succeed his cousin Harthacnut (from whom he claimed he also had a promise of the crown). A promise of succession to Sweyn would have defused the immediate situation, left Sweyn free to pursue his warfare with Magnus and Harald Hardrada, and enabled Edward to stand down his fleet and stop levying the unpopular Danegeld. If he made the undertaking (and he seems to have been remarkably free with promises of the crown, which in fact he had no right to give), he probably never expected to have to honour it. The life expectancy of the Danish kings was poor.

The claims of Harald Hardrada and Sweyn Estrithson should be seen in the context of eleventh-century Scandinavia. Even a brief scrutiny of the history of Denmark, Norway and Sweden around this time would be enough to show that constitutional propriety and primogeniture played little part in the choice of their kings; even a remote connection with a previous monarch was sufficient to support a claim, and the outcomes were usually decided by force, not justice. The success of Cnut was still vividly remembered by the English. This should be borne in mind when considering the claims of the next contestant for the throne of England, who was also, if more remotely, of Scandinavian origin.

The claim of William of Normandy was based on the marriage of his great-aunt, Emma, to King Æthelred. This, he contended, made him Edward's kinsman and certainly he was cousin to the king at one remove, though not in the legitimate line of succession. In addition his family had given shelter to Emma, her husband Æthelred and her children when they were exiled from England, though, as has been noted, there is no evidence that any grant of land was ever made to Edward and Alfred while they were exiles in Normandy. In gratitude for the generosity of Normandy, William's chroniclers allege, and in recognition of the outstanding abilities and merits of William himself and of the close and loving friendship between them, Edward promised him the succession when he returned to England. In the words of William of Poitiers:

> it was also through [William's] support and counsel that, on the death of Harthacnut, Edward was at last crowned and placed on his father's throne, a distinction of which he was most worthy, as much through his wisdom and outstanding moral worth as by his ancient lineage. For the English, when they had discussed the question, agreed that William's arguments were the best, and acquiesced in the just request of his envoys to avoid experiencing the might of the Normans.[ix]

It may be asked how close and loving a friendship could be between a man of forty and a boy of thirteen, how much of the might of Normandy could have been spared from its own problems in 1041 for Edward's assistance (had it been needed, which it was not), or how Edward managed to detect in the beleaguered boy duke of Normandy the outstanding abilities that fitted him for kingship; when Edward left Normandy, the prospects of William surviving his minority and the many plots against him long enough to take control of Normandy were remote. It is, of course, perfectly possible to imagine a situation in which a middle-aged man might say lightly to a child cousin that he should be his heir, especially if there was then little prospect of there being a throne to inherit or of the child surviving long enough to inherit it. It was William's contention that the promise was made, was made seriously and was renewed after Edward succeeded to the throne. If so, the timing of this renewal is problematic.

It has usually been assumed that the northern version of the Anglo-Saxon Chronicle (D) was right in stating that William came on some sort of state visit to England in 1051, after the outlawry of the Godwin family in September, and that this was the occasion of the promise, though it should be noted that William's biographer, D. C. Douglas, has suggested that this entry in the Chronicle may have been a late interpolation; he points out that the surviving manuscript of D is almost certainly post-1100 and thus must have been copied from another version, now lost.[x] There are, however, grave difficulties with this 1051 scenario. Setting aside the peculiarity of this reference in the version of the Chronicle furthest from the scene of events in the south, why did the two main Norman chroniclers (William of Jumièges and William of Poitiers) fail to mention the visit? Both were anxious to include in their accounts anything that tended to strengthen William's claim. It has been suggested that they omitted it because it showed William as a suitor to Edward, which would have demeaned him. This seems most improbable. There would have been nothing demeaning in the ruler of Normandy paying a state visit to his cousin in England and if, while he was there, the English king had decided to make him his heir, this would have given him more, not less, prestige and would have been no more than they claimed had already happened in Normandy.

There is then the claim of William of Poitiers that the king's promise was formally witnessed by the most important men in England, namely Siward of Northumbria, Leofric of Mercia, Godwin of Wessex and Stigand, Archbishop of Canterbury. There was no occasion, certainly not in 1051, when all these people could have been assembled at court holding these particular offices. In late 1051 Earl Godwin was in exile, and it was not Stigand who was Archbishop of Canterbury but the Norman Robert of Jumièges, who might indeed have been happy to witness such a promise; it is highly unlikely that either Siward or Leofric would have been. Rumours of such an intention or such a promise might well explain why both Siward and Leofric declined to oppose Godwin's return in the following year, since he of all of them had most strongly opposed the Norman faction at court. If, on the other hand, such a promise had been publicly given and formally witnessed, as this account implies, it is even more incredible that there should be no record of it in any of the English sources. The only point in favour of this extraordinary story is the indication, oblique though it is, that William of Poitiers realized that the crown was not Edward's to give away on his own whim. The alleged assent of the foremost men of the kingdom might be regarded as an earnest of the Witan's reaction later on. It has been suggested that Edward's promise might have been witnessed in two stages, at the time he gave it by Leofric and Siward and later, in 1052, by Godwin and Stigand as a condition of Godwin's reinstatement, and that this would account for Godwin giving hostages at this point, but the idea is unconvincing.[xi] Godwin, when he returned, was in a position of strength; he would not have needed to make such a concession.

There is also the allegation that at this time Edward gave hostages to William as a pledge of his promise; the hostages are named as Wulfnoth, the youngest son of Earl Godwin, and Hakon, the son of Godwin's eldest son, Sweyn. Nothing is known of Hakon. Wulfnoth certainly did pass into William's hands as a hostage at some stage, since he spent his life in Norman captivity, was released by William on his deathbed and promptly re-imprisoned by his son William Rufus. But at what stage and why he was handed over is not clear. It is highly unlikely to have been in 1051. At that date, he must have been little more than a boy, and it is very improbable that Godwin, removing all his family to exile in Flanders in September 1051, should have overlooked this one son or obliged Edward by leaving him to become a hostage. However, the Chronicle (E) does say that when the king and Godwin were reconciled in 1052, they exchanged hostages, a normal procedure on such an occasion; this is the most likely time for Wulfnoth and Hakon to have been handed over and sent by Edward to Normandy for safe-keeping. The idea that the hostages were given to William by Edward in 1051 in support of his promise is in any case a little ridiculous – and if his promise was, as maintained by the Normans, witnessed by all the chief men in the kingdom, why only Godwin family hostages? Where were the hostages, for example, from the family of Leofric? In any case, a man would hardly be expected to give hostages to another on whom he was conferring a massive favour; and even if he did, it would normally be a two-way affair; there is no indication of any hostages being given by William to Edward.

The most convincing argument against William's visit in 1051, however, is William's own situation in Normandy. He had succeeded his father as Duke of Normandy in 1035 at the age of seven, on the death of Duke Robert who was returning from pilgrimage to Jerusalem, and had had a troubled minority, mainly through the resentment of legitimate adult kinsmen who objected to the succession of a bastard child, partly through the ambition of those who aspired to dominance of the duchy through the guardianship of the child duke. Several of those originally appointed his guardians met violent or suspicious deaths, and there was more than one attempt on his own life. During his minority, all order and prosperity in the duchy disintegrated. The idea that William was in any way responsible for Edward's return to the English throne, as his chroniclers claimed, can hardly be borne out by the situation in which the thirteen-year-old duke found himself in 1041. In 1046 he was confronted by a rebellion raised by his cousin, Guy of Brionne, a grandson of Duke Richard II, who was strongly supported by many of the Norman nobility. William was forced to flee and to ask for the help of his overlord, King Henry of France, under whose leadership he confronted and defeated the rebels at the battle of Val-ès-Dune in 1047. It was his effective coming of age. Guy took refuge in his castle of Brionne, and it took William about three years to eject and banish him. In the meantime, King Henry demanded his *quid pro quo* in the form of William's help against another turbulent vassal, Geoffrey Martel, Count of Anjou. William provided the help, but found himself, in consequence, with another dangerous enemy to the south of him in the form of Martel, who lost little time in challenging him. He was joined in this by King Henry who had clearly decided that William was, after all, even more dangerous than Martel. From 1050 onwards, William was under constant threat from both. If his biographer, D. C. Douglas, is correct, in 1051 he was occupied with the sieges of Alençon and Domfront on his frontier, and also with marrying the Count of Flanders' daughter, Matilda, a matter of much delicate negotiation since they were declared by the Church to be within the prohibited degrees of affinity. His dealings with the defenders of Alençon and Domfront were less delicate; the former defied him by beating pelts over the battlements in allusion to his birth as the bastard of a tanner's daughter. William retaliated by chopping off their hands and feet when the castle eventually capitulated. The sieges of Alençon and Domfront are placed by Douglas in the autumn and winter of 1051, precisely the time at which the visit to England would have taken place.[xii] William must also have been aware that he was likely in the near future to face another family rebellion closer to home from his uncle, the Count of Arques; the rebellion eventually broke out in 1052 or 1053, supported by the King of France and by a powerful coalition of neighbouring princes. It has been suggested that William's English ambitions and the possibility of a shift in the balance of power in France if he won the English throne had alarmed other northern French rulers. The Count of Arques' rebellion was crushed and Arques himself exiled for life. From that date, however, until Martel and the king both died in 1060, William was under constant attack from both of them. The idea that in the midst of these threats to his rule, actual or threatened, William would have contemplated leaving his duchy undefended for long enough to pay a visit to his cousin in England, even with the possibility that he might receive the promise of a throne in the course of it, is quite simply incredible. There was no Channel tunnel in the mid-eleventh century; if William had come to England in late 1051, he ran the risk of being trapped there by contrary winds for as long as he was prevented in 1066 from launching his invasion fleet. He could not be sure of getting home in a hurry if Martel or the French king, both constantly on the lookout for an opportunity to attack, broke his borders. In 1051 Edward, though by contemporary standards an elderly man, was in good health. He hunted regularly and led an active life. There was no imminent likelihood of his death. William, constantly in the battlefield, was much more at risk. Never a man to act without careful consideration, he would have been insane to risk his bird in the hand (Normandy) for the possibility of a bird in the bush (England) at this particular juncture. Promises, after all, like piecrusts, are made to be broken. Edward can hardly have been pleased by William's marriage to the daughter of a man whom he regarded as an enemy and hostile to England; and his action in sending into Hungary so shortly afterwards to urge the return of Edward the Exile indicates clearly that, whether or not he had made any promises to William in the past, he was prepared to break them in the interests of a peaceful succession that would be acceptable to his councillors.

There is another way in which a promise to William might have been conveyed. In 1051 Robert of Jumièges succeeded Eadsige as Archbishop of Canterbury and set off for Rome to collect his pallium from the Pope. The pallium, a narrow band of white lamb's wool, was bestowed on metropolitans and primates by the Holy See and was the symbol of the power delegated to them by the Pope. (In the Middle Ages, popes made a handsome income from the fees they charged recipients for it.) It has been suggested that Robert travelled south via Normandy, perhaps with a verbal message from Edward to William, and according to William of Jumièges this was what happened. It is even possible that he might have ventriloquized one, in a spirit of wishful thinking. However, it is relevant to note that there is absolutely no evidence whatsoever on the English side of any party supporting a Norman successor, although the question of the succession must have been becoming more urgent every year. The first indication of any action in the matter is the move to repatriate Edward the Exile.

The final claimant to the throne was, of course, Harold Godwinson. It is fairly clear that William had set his sights on the English crown quite early in his career; it is less certain when Harold realized that he could be a contender, possibly not until after the death of Edward the Exile, since he appears to have supported and indeed negotiated for his return to England. He may not even have thought of it then. He might well have thought that he could re-enact the part played by the hero of the Old English epic poem *Beowulf* who, after the death of his lord, King Hygelac, acted as guardian to Hygelac's youthful son Heardred until he came of age. As guardian to Edgar during his minority, his own position would be assured and he would be well placed to defend the kingdom and, indeed, the interests of the Godwin family. At some time, however, the idea of his own succession must have occurred to him and to others. In terms of blood lineage, he had, of course, no possible claim, and never pretended to any. None the less, even in these terms, his claim was better than William's. William was the great-nephew of a woman who had married a reigning king; Harold was the brother of a woman who had married a reigning king. Neither of them had a drop of English royal blood. It has been suggested that Harold might have made a claim through his Danish blood, because his mother was a kinswoman of Cnut; but this claim would depend on the rather doubtful proposition that Edward had succeeded to the English throne as half-brother of Harthacnut who had brought him back from exile, not as son of Æthelred. Even if this were to be allowed, his cousin, Sweyn Estrithson, had a far more direct claim through the Danish line. Apart from blood lineage, Harold had the advantage of having been born in wedlock. The conditions for kingship had been set out at an ecclesiastical synod held in England in the presence of papal legates in 786, and specified that 'Kings are to be lawfully chosen by the priests and elders of the people, and are not to be those begotten in adultery or incest'. These conditions had not always been observed in the past; there had, for example, been considerable doubt over the legality of Edward the Elder's marriage to his first wife, Ecgwynn, and thus over the legitimacy of Athelstan, but when such doubts were ignored, it was usually for good reasons.

Harold's chief claim, however, was not of blood or legitimacy; it was that he was 'lawfully chosen'. In a situation in which the only remaining member of the West Saxon blood line was a boy, and the kingdom faced the likelihood of invasion as in the days of Alfred and his immediate successors, the elders of the people looked for a candidate who had both the administrative ability and the military experience to defend the country. In 1066 the elders of the people, personified by the Witan, faced with the prospect of invasion on two fronts, had urgent need to find such a candidate. Harold qualified on both counts. He had to all intents and purposes ruled England efficiently as *subregulus* or under-king for many years (after the death of Gruffydd following Harold's Welsh campaign, the Welsh swore fealty and obedience jointly to Edward and Harold); and he was beyond question the most experienced and able military commander in the country. He also appears to have been genuinely popular. The Waltham chronicler (admittedly probably as biased in one direction as William of Poitiers was in the other, but writing after the conquest when Harold had already been defeated and praise of him was not encouraged) records that he was elected king by unanimous consent 'for there was no one in the land more knowledgeable, more vigorous in arms, wiser in the laws of the land or more highly regarded for his prowess of every kind.'[xiii] The more unbiased Anglo-Saxon Chronicle (C and D) recorded his election in terms that are not those in which one describes a usurper, though these, like the Waltham Chronicle, must have been written after Hastings:

> And the wise king entrusted that kingdom to the high-
> ranking man, Harold himself, the noble earl, who at all
> times faithfully obeyed his lord in word and deed,
> neglecting nothing of which the king had need; and here
> Harold was hallowed as king. And he enjoyed little
> stillness while he held the kingdom.

In the context of the times, and in a situation where the royal line had failed, his succession in England was no more irregular than that of Hugh Capet to the throne of France on the collapse of the Carolingian monarchy some years earlier. Hugh Capet was crowned on the recommendation of Archbishop Adalbéron:

> Crown the Duke. He is most illustrious by his exploits,
> his nobility, his forces. The throne is not acquired by
> hereditary right; no one should be raised to it unless
> distinguished not only for nobility of birth but for the
> goodness of his soul.

Harold was already virtual King of England, to much the same extent that Hugh Capet had been virtual King of France in 987. William, who received news regularly from England, would have been aware for some time that Harold was likely to pose an obstacle to his ambition. The question of how to circumvent that obstacle must have exercised him greatly. He could hardly have hoped for the accident that delivered Harold into his hands.

The short story of the accident (which is only recorded in the Norman sources, though its essence has not been seriously challenged) was that Harold crossed the Channel, probably but not certainly in 1064, for an unknown reason. It has been suggested[xiv] that the trip took place in late 1065, immediately after the exile of Tostig, on the grounds that William of Poitiers says that at this stage the king was very near death. Setting aside William of Poitiers' doubtful veracity, Harold would have been extremely unlikely either to go on a pleasure trip or to make a diplomatic visit to Normandy to promise the crown to William when there had just been a major insurrection in England, as in 1065, and the king was very near death, especially if, as is assumed, he had designs on the crown himself by this time. The most reliable evidence indicates that Edward's final illness began as a result of the exile of Tostig in 1065; after that, Harold would have been as mad to leave England as William would have been to leave Normandy in 1051, even if there had, in practical terms, been time to fit such a visit in between Tostig's exile at the beginning of November 1065 and the king's death on 5 January 1066. 1064, when he vanishes temporarily from the English chronicles altogether, is a much more likely date.

At all events, by storm or miscalculation, he was cast up on the coast of Ponthieu. The inhabitants of Ponthieu were well known as wreckers; this is confirmed even by William of Poitiers. There were many stories that lights were frequently shown at dangerous points of the coast to mislead sailors, since ships that were wrecked in their territory were legal prey and the sailors could be imprisoned or tortured for vast sums in ransom. Whether by storm or misleading lights, Harold's ship foundered, and he and his companions were captured; he might have been able to extricate himself by payment of a ransom if one of his captors had not recognized him and betrayed him to the Count of Ponthieu, who immediately realized that in him he had a prize far out of the common and incarcerated him and his men in a dungeon. Someone (possibly one of Harold's men, he is depicted in the Bayeux Tapestry as moustached, the infallible sign of an Englishman) went to the neighbouring duchy of Normandy and told the duke, who was the Count of Ponthieu's overlord, what had happened. William immediately ordered Guy of Ponthieu to hand Harold and his men over to him. He was rewarded by William with cash and land. Harold remained in Normandy for some time, was treated with honour by the duke, campaigned with him in Brittany (where, with great heroism, he rescued two of William's soldiers from the quicksands), and left again for England after swearing an oath on the bones of the saints that he would support William's claim to the English throne after Edward's death. This, at least, is the version of the Norman chroniclers and of the Bayeux Tapestry.

Many explanations have been offered as to why Harold happened to be crossing the Channel at this particular moment. The Norman version (William of Poitiers) was that he was sent by King Edward to confirm his promise of the throne to the duke and did so voluntarily. An English version (Eadmer) is that he went on his own initiative to try to retrieve his brother and nephew who had been handed over to the duke as hostages. According to Eadmer, he went against the advice of the king, who warned him not to trust William. In the event he retrieved his nephew Hakon (of whom nothing is known and whose very existence is slightly suspect) but not his brother Wulfnoth, who remained in William's custody. Yet another version is that he had gone sailing for diversion with no intention of going to Normandy, and had been caught and blown ashore by a storm. According to Henry of Huntingdon, he was on his way to Flanders, not Normandy; this plausible idea is not corroborated elsewhere. There is no possibility now of discovering the truth. One can only make a guess at the likelihoods. There is very little probability in the idea that he was sent by Edward to convey a promise and swear an oath that would have been repugnant to him. After the king, he was the most powerful man in the kingdom; if Edward had asked him to do such a thing, he would have had little difficulty in refusing or procrastinating. One modern apologist for William has offered the rather desperate explanation that he knew that if he refused to go, Edward would have sent his brother Tostig in his place.[xv] A message or an oath from Tostig, who had no support in England, would have been of little use to William; and moreover, if Harold were prepared to break his own oath on holy relics in his pursuit of the crown, he would surely have had few scruples about ignoring his brother's. It would, in fact, have been very much better from Harold's point of view that Tostig should have gone and sworn oaths. If Harold proposed to sail into Normandy with the intention of demanding Edward's hostages back, he was more naive and trusting than history shows him to have been; William's ambitions must have been common knowledge by this time, and Harold is described in the *Vita Ædwardi* as having made use of his foreign travels to acquire a detailed knowledge of European politics, with the comment that he had such an exhaustive knowledge of European princes that he could not be deceived by any of their proposals.[xvi] The idea that he was blown off course during a sailing trip is at least believable.

It is here, for the first time, that some help may be derived from the Bayeux Tapestry, for it begins at this point in the story. The first panel or frame shows King Edward sitting in his chair of state, holding his sceptre and apparently conversing affably with two men standing beside him. The taller and more impressive of these is not named but is assumed to be Harold, since in the next panel Harold is shown setting off for Bosham with his men. Harold's conversation with the king seems to be amicable. This is the image that has been interpreted as Edward instructing Harold to travel to Normandy to confirm his promise to William. But there is absolutely nothing in the picture or the text to confirm this. There is, in fact, no text over the picture, which would as well fit any of the other explanations for his voyage; Harold might be asking permission to go on a fishing or hunting trip or to Flanders or proposing to go to redeem the hostages, though in that case the expression on the king's face would perhaps be more concerned or anxious. If the mission were as important as the designation of the king's successor, it would surely have been glossed; it would, after all, have been the foundation of the whole Norman claim.

The next few panels follow the standard version of the story: Harold arrives at Bosham, where there was a family manor, prays at the church there, eats and drinks with his companions, boards the ship and, with the sails 'full of wind', comes into the territory of Count Guy. Here he is arrested by Guy's men and taken to Beaurain. There is no explicit mention of a storm, though the wind in the sails might be interpreted that way[xvii]. The narrative then shows his transfer to the hands of William, his campaign with William in Brittany (including his rescue of two of William's men from the quicksands) and finally the most important scene, the swearing of an oath to William. According to William of

Poitiers, who alone gives a detailed account, this oath consisted of undertakings to support William's claim to the throne, to act for him in England until the king's death, to fortify Dover and other places that William would specify for the duke's use and garrison them with Norman knights whom Harold would maintain, to marry the duke's daughter and to send his sister into Normandy to marry a Norman. Immediately after this, he is shown returning home to England, where he has another interview with the king – but a very different king this time. He is drawn and haggard, the finger extended towards Harold no longer indicating merely conversation but rather admonition or accusation. Harold for his part is apologetic and contrite, his head bowed, his hands extended in an exculpatory gesture. It is impossible to misread this scene: the king has heard something that worries and distresses him greatly, Harold is apologizing and excusing himself. If Harold had gone in the first place to confirm promises and make vows on the king's behalf, why should he be apologizing? We have seen him do this. The only obvious answer is that he did not go to do this, but he has, for whatever reason, sworn a vow and in so doing has landed himself in bad trouble with his king. It is interesting that, having portrayed the situation so graphically, the designer has not attempted to explain it; the legend overhead simply says 'he [i.e. Harold] came to King Edward'. It is here, more than anywhere else, that the Tapestry is most ambiguous.

The only explanation that makes sense of everything is that offered by the monk Eadmer. According to him, Harold wanted to go to redeem the family hostages in Normandy and asked permission from the king to do so. The king apparently gave this reluctantly, but warned him that he would only bring misfortune on the whole kingdom and discredit upon himself, for 'I know that the Duke is not so simple as to be at all inclined to give them up to you unless he foresees that in doing so he will secure some great advantage to himself.'[xviii]

The duke was not simple and he did indeed gain great advantage for himself. Without the oath sworn and broken by Harold, it is highly improbable that the Vatican could have been persuaded to turn an unprovoked attack on a neighbouring independent and peaceful kingdom into a holy war against a perjurer (if indeed it did, as we shall see in due course). And without papal backing, William's success would have been much less likely.

It is extremely improbable that Harold would willingly and freely have sworn to the conditions recorded by William of Poitiers; as has been noted by previous historians, at least two of them would have amounted to treason against the present king. On the other hand, he was in a desperately precarious situation. As Eadmer points out, he was in danger whichever way he turned. He cannot have been unaware that his recent host, Guy of Ponthieu, had been captured by William after the battle of Mortemer and had been held incarcerated in Normandy for two years until he freed himself by swearing allegiance to the duke and accepting him as his overlord; nor that after William's recent unprovoked conquest of Maine, the rival claimants, Count Walter and his wife (also possible claimants to the throne of England and with a much stronger claim than William's), had died by poison in his custody. However courteously entertained at the Norman court so far, he was in fact a prisoner, and if he refused to swear, his conditions were likely to become less comfortable. And as the effective deputy king of England, his prolonged absence would be disastrous. If he took the oath, he probably did so relying on the generally accepted belief that a forced oath was not regarded as binding. He might also have remembered Alfred's law (the very first in his code) that, 'If a man is wrongfully constrained to promise either to betray his lord or to aid an unlawful undertaking, then it is better to be false to the promise than to fulfil it.' No wonder that on his return the king is reported by Eadmer as saying reproachfully, 'Did I not tell you that I knew William and that your going might bring untold calamity upon this kingdom?'[xix] Such an explanation makes perfect sense of the expression on the king's face in the Tapestry and of Harold's abject stance.

In considering this, one may also bear in mind the close connection that both the Tapestry and Eadmer had with Canterbury (Eadmer certainly and the Tapestry probably), and the possibility of some now unknown connection between the two accounts and also, of course, the fact that Eadmer was writing with the benefit of hindsight. If no hostages were ever given to William by Edward (we only have William of Poitiers' word that they were), and Wulfnoth was imprisoned by William on a different or later occasion, then Eadmer's version would fall to the ground. But there may be reasons for giving some credence to Eadmer's account. It has been suggested by Harold's biographer, Ian W. Walker, that Bishop Æthelric of Sussex, who was consulted by Eadmer over his life of St Dunstan, may well have been the Æthelric of Christ Church, Canterbury, whose election as archbishop was rejected by King Edward in 1050 in favour of Robert of Jumièges. If so, he was a relation of the Godwin family; and if so, this connection would have allowed Eadmer access to a relative of Harold's when he wrote his account of the events of 1064, giving his version some authority.[xx] At the very least it implies the existence in Canterbury, and possibly further afield, of a reasonably plausible account of events that might reconcile Eadmer's history with the Tapestry.

Whichever version comes nearest the truth, William appears to have equipped himself in advance with, according to Goebbels, the best ingredient for propaganda – the big lie consistently told: that the kingdom had been promised to him by King Edward (possibly not altogether a lie but certainly not proved and in any case not a valid promise), and that Harold had freely and voluntarily sworn on the bones of the saints to uphold his claim to it. William was to use his advantage skilfully.

THE PRIZE

I t is impossible to understand the determination with which the various contenders pursued their claims without understanding the value of the prize for which they were competing. The civilization and culture that in the eleventh century distinguished England from her European neighbours were less important to them than her wealth, which was legendary and colossal, even after the Viking depredations of Æthelred's reign. Looking back from this distance in time, it is easy to think of Anglo-Saxon England as a remote, comparatively brief and homogeneous phase of history, in much the same way that we think of Tudor or Victorian England. This would be to underrate its duration and its significance. The Anglo-Saxons ruled England for six centuries, as long as from the Middle Ages to the present day, about as long as the duration of the Roman Empire, a period broken only by the twenty-five-year kingship of Cnut and his sons. Naturally, during these six centuries, much changed, and the barbaric paganism of the original settlers evolved relatively peacefully into the rich, sophisticated, Christian kingdom of 1066, of which it has been said that 'the most important economic developments before the Industrial Revolution took place in the later Anglo-Saxon period'.[xxi] In the confusion of Dark Age Europe, and unlike the *parvenu* Norman dukedom founded in 911,

England stood out among other European states for its antiquity, its long-established line of kings, most of them highly effective rulers, its well-developed governmental systems, its stable and well-regulated currency and, in consequence, its thriving economy and prosperity.

It was conspicuous, too, eventually, for another characteristic: its unity. How much of this was due to the fact that it was, to all intents and purposes, an island state is difficult to assess; the fact is that, in comparison with other western European states of the time, such as proto-France or Germany, it was a united and self-conscious nation state. The English king's writ in the eleventh century ran fairly consistently throughout his realm, admittedly less strongly in the north towards the Scottish border, though the legal concessions allowed in the Danelaw were more apparent than significant. By contrast, the French king (or king of the western Franks, as he was more correctly known at this date) had real authority over an area little larger than the Ile de France, and was hemmed in on all sides by vassals who may technically have owed him allegiance but who in fact governed (and contended among themselves) as independent sovereigns in their own lands such as Anjou, Maine, Blois, Ponthieu and Normandy. The English state may have started in the fifth century as a conglomeration of independent kingdoms known loosely as the Saxon Heptarchy; but it was a more homogeneous body than has always been recognized, in which the various petty kingdoms very soon had more in common with each other than with either the former British races whom they encountered on arrival or with the continental districts from which they had come. They quickly came to share a language that would have been in some degree intelligible in any of them. The Venerable Bede, born in the seventh century, described the languages of Britain as English,

British (that is, Welsh), Scots, Pictish and Latin; he did not subdivide English into West Saxon, Mercian, Northumbrian or Kentish. Individual kingdoms expanded or shrank by a natural process of ebb and flow. Every now and then, one particularly strong ruler would manage to assert his power over his peers and achieve the slightly legendary title of *Bretwalda* or ruler of all Britain; this usually ceased at his death and the title lapsed until a successor or a rival was strong enough to claim it. Inter-marriages between the different royal houses produced a network of alliances and kinships that meant there was more to connect the various kingdoms than to separate them. The importance of the conversion of the English and the developing institutions of the Church can hardly be overestimated. Monasteries were being founded the length and breadth of England, all working to the same rule, with monks and abbots (many of them from the most powerful and noble families in the country) moving between them; the importance of their unifying role is obvious, as was that of the metropolitan sees of Canterbury and York.

The ninth-century Viking invasions also played an important part in breaking down what by that time remained of the old divisions and pushing the various constituent parts of the country together. To begin with, it seemed that the old Anglo-Saxon England would be submerged beneath the Scandinavian invaders; but after the fight-back by Alfred and his successors, England in more or less its eleventh-century form had emerged with Wessex predominant, and Alfred's grandson, King Athelstan, could without exaggeration call himself king of all England. It is said that King Edgar, Athelstan's nephew, made a point of circum-navigating his entire kingdom every year by sea. If he did, he must have taken in Scotland and Wales as well, over which the English kings rarely had more than a nominal supremacy, but certainly the King of Scotland and Kings of Wales were among the eight subject kings who reputedly rowed Edgar on the river Dee at his coronation. More practically, he promoted the unity of his kingdom by introducing a uniform currency all over England that he alone controlled and that was withdrawn periodically, usually every five or six years, and replaced by another. Apart from providing a significant source of royal revenue for himself and his successors, since all moneyers had to buy the new dies from the king when this happened, this reform promoted the development of the economy at home and abroad, where English coins were much respected. This was to be one of the English customs that the Conqueror did not abolish.

Thus, when the Viking raids resumed in the tenth century, the raiders found a united country in which the Byrhtnoth who confronted them at Maldon in 991 may have been a nobleman of the former kingdom of the East Saxons but who announced himself to them as 'Æthelred's earl', fighting to protect the West Saxon Æthelred's England, his land and his people, with an army that included at least one Mercian and one Northumbrian, and representatives of all the social classes of England, united in a determination to defend their country. If, as has been suggested, *The Battle of Maldon* was not written until about thirty years after the battle, it looks even more like a deliberate attempt to portray the defence of a kingdom united in race and class. It throws into sad contrast the verdict of the Anglo-Saxon Chronicle in 1010, later in the reign of Æthelred, when the demoralization of the country had led to a situation in which 'no shire would any longer help its neighbour'.

Because of the length of time that the Anglo-Saxon rule lasted, it was naturally not the same throughout, but there were, none the less, consistent threads running through the period. The kingdoms that the seventh-century Ine and the tenth-century Athelstan ruled were indeed very different in many respects, but those over which Athelstan and Edward the Confessor ruled were not in essence very dissimilar. The Domesday Book (1086), one of William's most famous (and, it must be said, most valuable) achievements, aimed to take a snapshot picture of England 'on the day King Edward was alive and dead', 5 January 1066; many of the institutions that it records as having existed then and that survived the conquest have been shown to go far back in history, many of them to a time well before King Alfred or even King Ine. It has been surmised that some of the most important elements of them, for example the system of hundreds, the local government units into which the shires were broken down for administrative and tax purposes, may well go back to a common Indo-European culture, for traces of it have been noted in Carolingian France also. Many of them survived far into the future as well. The shire structure itself continued through the conquest unaltered and untampered with until 1974. A retiring prime minister, resigning his parliamentary seat in the early years of the twenty-first century, still had to apply for the stewardship of the Chiltern hundreds of Stoke, Desborough and Burnham in Buckinghamshire.

The system of justice meant that wherever a man lived, he was rarely in a district so remote that he did not have access to a court of law: the king's court, the shire court, the hundred court. The involvement of the different ranks of the people in the different levels of the national administration of justice was also a unifying factor, and gave the public at large a voice in national affairs that could never have been imagined in, say, Normandy during the reign of autocrats such as Duke William or his father. There were written law-codes in England from the time of King Æthelberht of Kent in the sixth century, and there are many hints between the times of Æthelberht and Edward the Confessor that not even the king could be regarded as being above the law (not least the agreement between Æthelred and his people that he would be accepted back as king provided he ruled better). In considering why the Angevin kings were to prove more effective legislators in England than in their homeland of Anjou, Patrick Wormald suggests that this could be because in the tenth and eleventh centuries, English kings had laid down the law as no other western rulers did.[xxii] Henry II, he points out, made law like no other twelfth-century king because he inherited a system of royal justice that was already uniquely well developed and active. There had never been any written law-code in Normandy. It has been said that

> the English kings, like the Carolingians but unlike most
> of the Carolingians' successors, maintained a system of
> rule in which their contact, via public courts, with a
> fairly large number of free classes mattered for them,
> and for those classes. That those courts and classes
> survived the Conquest may well have done much to
> determine the later history of England.[xxiii]

It has been estimated that in Anglo-Saxon England there were rarely more than two layers of lordship between the yeoman and his king. A situation in which King Alfred could give judgement in a case while he was in his chamber washing his hands was recorded for posterity not because it was unusual but because it was habitual – one of the plaintiffs had appealed to the king from the local shire or hundred court.[xxiv] It is true that in the days of Alfred's descendants, particularly during the reign of Æthelred when the need to pay Danegeld led to the frequent levying of extra taxes, this independence of the peasant-farmer was to some extent eroded, probably in the main because of the increasing difficulty smallholders experienced in maintaining themselves. A bad harvest could bring them to the verge of starvation; a Danish raid could reduce them overnight to beggary. It made sense in such cases for a smallholder to trade in his nominal independence for the security of binding himself and the land that he had inherited in some form of servitude to a lord who was able to protect or maintain him. There is little doubt, however, that the process was accelerated and, to some extent, brutalized by the conquest; Stenton has noted that 'many peasants who in 1066 had been holding land immediately of the king, or as the voluntary dependents of other magnates, are represented in Domesday Book by *villani* [serfs] on the estates of Norman lords.'[xxv]

Moreover, the sophisticated system of land tenure in England meant that the kings always knew exactly what they could count on in terms of revenue and fighting men, and their subjects knew what their liabilities were as precisely. It has been calculated that in the whole of England, there was not a scrap of land unaccounted for in the assessment system. Each hundred was broken down into so many hides of land (carucates in the Danelaw, sulungs in Kent). Theoretically, the hide was originally the amount of land sufficient for a peasant family to live on, but very soon the hide ceased to have any relationship to a specific area of land (just as the modern pound has ceased to have any relationship to a specific weight of gold) and became simply a unit of assessment, so that hides in different parts of the country might be assessed differently, often according to the wealth or productivity of the area. A man's ownership of, say, five hides of land might typically mean that he was liable for so much in taxes, for the provision of a fighting man with all his equipment for a specified number of days a year when the king needed him for the defence of the realm, and for various other services. Such services might include, depending on the owner's rank, duties of hospitality and escort to the king or his family, food rent (the laws of Ine tell us that the food rent from a ten-hide estate should be ten vats of honey, three hundred loaves, twelve ambers of Welsh ale, thirty of clear ale, two full-grown cows or ten wethers, ten geese, twenty hams, ten cheeses, an amber of butter, five salmon, twenty pounds of fodder and a hundred eels) and other miscellaneous services such as maintenance of hedges. Some of these might be remitted in special circumstances; the three services that were almost never remitted, whether the land were owned by a layman or the Church, were military service, the construction and maintenance of the country's fortifications and bridge-building. It was this efficient system of assessment that made it possible for Æthelred to raise quickly as extra taxes the vast sums of money that were needed to pay off the Danes between 991 and 1016. It is hardly surprising that they kept coming back for more.

However efficient the tax-collecting system, it would hardly have worked if the money had not been there to be collected. Despite the frequent plundering raids, England was known to be wealthy – indeed, its notorious wealth had much to do with the frequency of the raids. Through the six centuries of its existence, the Anglo-Saxon kingdom had been a trading nation, but it had also achieved renown in various kinds of manufacture. Much of the detail of what the country once produced and contained is still obscure, despite recent archaeological research, and will no doubt remain so because by its nature it was perishable; the remaining archival evidence indicates only a fragment of what must once have existed. But there is enough information in the surviving letters, wills and deeds to give some idea of what people produced and had to dispose of. The evidence of the sheer amount of bullion in the country is impressive, without considering its artistry which, by all accounts, was equally so. As far as imports are concerned, especially those made of precious metals, even William of Poitiers, no friend to the English, and a man who believed that the sooner English treasures were sanitized by passing into Norman hands the better, noted the country's wealth:

> To this most fertile land merchants used to bring added wealth in imported riches. Treasures remarkable for their number and kind and workmanship had been amassed there, either to be kept for the empty enjoyment of avarice, or to be squandered shamefully in English luxury.[xxvi]

If we consider merely the Sutton Hoo treasure of c.650, the greatest find yet discovered, we are looking at imports from Byzantium, the Mediterranean, Egypt and Sweden at the very least, and at jewellery that may well have been made in Kent, a known centre for this particular kind of fine workmanship. Frequent references in the various codes of laws drawn up by successive kings make it clear how important trade was to the country and how vital they considered it to be that foreign merchants should be protected and their trade properly regulated.

Commerce was not the only channel through which foreign goods entered the kingdom. The diplomatic and marriage alliances that the English kings had built up throughout Europe meant that there were many ways in which trade could be promoted, and goods and gifts of great value passed backwards and forwards. Dorothy Whitelock[xxvii] quotes an impressive list of the valuable gifts sent by Hugh, Duke of the Franks, to King

Athelstan when he asked for the hand of Athelstan's half-sister Eadhild in marriage.^{xxviii} The eldest son of King Æthelred who predeceased his father, another Athelstan, left to his brother, Edmund Ironside, 'the sword which King Offa owned'. One can only conjecture whether this is the Hungarian sword known to have been sent by Charlemagne as a gift to the great Offa of Mercia; it may well have been. Swords were among the most treasured items a man could have, and were passed down as precious heirlooms, as was armour of all kinds, but swords had a particular value and were often decorated with quantities of gold and silver. Offa's sword was clearly priceless and Edmund Ironside put it to good use; but items of greater monetary though possibly less historical and symbolic value passed regularly between England and Europe.

It was not only through royal marriages and diplomatic dealings that there was contact with the outside world. One of the most striking things in the Anglo-Saxon Chronicle is the frequency with which pilgrimages to Rome (sometimes even to Jerusalem) are mentioned. Many of these were, naturally, journeys made by clerics; all archbishops had to go to Rome to collect the pallium or stole of office from the Pope. But many of them were made by lay people of all ranks, from kings downwards. The Chronicle also refers on several occasions to a special school or hostel in Rome built to accommodate the English pilgrims who went there (and, on some occasions, to accommodate their graves); and one of the achievements of Alfred and Cnut on their visits was to negotiate better terms for the English who made what was then an extremely hazardous journey. The itinerary of Archbishop Sigeric who fetched his pallium in 990 has survived, and records the names of seventy-nine stages on the journey from the Somme to Rome. On the assumption that each stage meant at least one night's lodging, the journey would have taken not less than three months in each direction, when the cross-Channel voyage and any necessary travel within England to the south coast are included. An archbishop would have been able to ride; those who had to go on foot probably took longer. Pilgrims normally made their wills before leaving. But those who returned brought goods of foreign workmanship with them, apart from any spiritual benefits.

Trade, however, internal as well as external, was the most important element in English prosperity in the late Anglo-Saxon period. It depended to a great extent on the maintenance of the means of communication. The three basic services that land-owners were rarely, if ever, excused contributed to this: if service in the fyrd or national host and the building and repair of fortifications were demanded primarily for purposes of the defence of the realm, the work on fortifications would have included the maintenance of roads, and the bridge-building requirement, though it might also have military aspects, was a significant contribution to the ability of merchants and goods to move around the kingdom. The evidence of caches of coins from the period all over England confirms that money did move around, for the vast majority of the coins found so far were minted miles from where they were dug up. One of the problems of knowing what was exported is the fact that, as already noted, much of it has perished during the last thousand years. Pottery tends to last better than other things and more pottery of the period has survived than anything else; if wood and leather and textiles were profitable articles of trade, as the written evidence suggests, few examples have been recovered to prove or illustrate it and we must rely on written sources for information. Henry of Huntingdon, writing about sixty years after the conquest (the basic conditions he described are unlikely to have changed significantly in the interim), tells us that, although little silver was mined in England, a large amount came into the country from Germany in payment for English exports (he mentions particularly fish, wool and cattle) so that there was more silver in England than in Germany itself.[xxix] As for the imports, the merchant in Ælfric's *Colloquy,* that delightful dialogue between a schoolmaster and his pupils, designed to be used to teach schoolboys Latin, gives us a list of what he brought back from overseas in the tenth century: purple garments and silks, precious stones and gold, various vestments and pigments, wine and oil, ivory, brass and tin (Cornwall must have seemed as remote as overseas to many Englishmen), sulphur and glass.[xxx]

Few artefacts, whether made in England or overseas, have survived from before 1066. This is easily understandable if we consider what hazards they were exposed to throughout the period of Anglo-Saxon civilization. Early Anglo-Saxon England, like most Dark Age European countries, was a violent place; and in the ninth century there was the first wave of Viking invasions, starting with the sack of Lindisfarne in 793 and continuing with the looting of most of the other English monasteries and churches for the precious metals and jewels with which they were lavishly and reverently endowed. What had been stripped was painstakingly restored during the comparative peace of the tenth century, only for the second wave of Danish depredation to begin in the 980s. Throughout the period, fire was a constant danger in a society that built largely in wood; textiles and books were especially vulnerable. The minsters in Canterbury (both of them) and York were all destroyed by fire shortly after the conquest. Christianity meant that burials from the age of the conversion onwards took place without grave goods such as those found at

Sutton Hoo, and where pagan burial sites did exist, they were frequently looted (that Sutton Hoo survived unlooted is, like the endurance of the Bayeux Tapestry, one of more inexplicable miracles). After the Norman Conquest English art treasures, particularly artefacts in gold and silver, were exported to Normandy and elsewhere in Europe on a scale unequalled in Europe until the days of the Nazi Property Transfer Office, no doubt to protect their original owners from the shameful luxury of which William of Poitiers complained. Finally, there was almost the worst act of vandalism of all, the dissolution of the monasteries at the Reformation, during which innumerable pieces of religious art were broken up or melted down. Items made of precious metals were always at risk of being melted down, either for refashioning in more modern styles or, more usually, for their cash value. William of Malmesbury records one such instance, this one not the responsibility of the Conqueror but of his heir, William Rufus:

> The bishops and abbots flocked to the court complaining about this outrage, pointing out that they were not able to meet such heavy taxation. . . To which, the officials of the court, replying as usual with angry expressions, said: 'Do you not have reliquaries made of gold and silver, full of the bones of dead men?' No other reply did they deign to give their petitioners. So, the latter, seeing the drift of the reply, stripped the reliquaries of the saints, despoiled the Crucifixes, melted down the chalices, not for the benefit of the poor but for the King's treasury. Almost everything which the holy frugality of their ancestors had preserved was consumed by the avarice of these extortioners.[xxxi]

Fortunately, there are records that give some idea of what England was once like. Dorothy Whitelock has given a good description of what the churches once had:

> . . .while the St Cuthbert stole and the Bayeux tapestry
> let us understand why English needlework was so prized
> on the Continent, it is the constant reference to precious
> objects – a cloak of remarkable purple, interwoven
> throughout with gold in the manner of a corselet, which
> was turned into a chasuble; robes of silk interwoven with
> precious work of gold and gems; a beautiful chasuble
> that shone like gold when worn in the house of the
> Lord; a chalice of gold flashing with gems 'as the
> heavens glow with blazing stars'; great candelabra, all of
> gold; images of the saints, covered with gold and silver
> and precious stones; and countless other treasures –
> vestments, altar-cloths, tapestries, dorsals, shrines,
> croziers, bells, etc. – which explains the great impression
> made on the Norman conquerors by the richness of the
> equipment of the English churches. We should never
> have guessed this without the aid of literary records.[xxxii]

Professor C. R. Dodwell has taken the trouble to go through all the written records and bring together the evidence they contain about Anglo-Saxon artefacts. His valuable book, *Anglo-Saxon Art*[xxxiii], has revealed an impressive amount of information about what used to exist, even if practically nothing of it has survived. It is clear from this that the average Anglo-Saxon, and even more the higher ranking ones, believed in conspicuous display. Anything that could be fashioned in gold was made of it. Objects that could not be made entirely of gold would at least be covered with it, like the ship presented by Earl Godwin to King Harthacnut, which not only had a gold-encrusted prow but was also equipped with eighty warriors, each of whom wore two gold arm-rings and had a partly gilded helmet, a sword with a gilded hilt, a battle-axe edged with gold and silver and a shield with gilded boss and studs. The description of Cnut's ships supports the evidence for this kind of display:

> So great, also, was the ornamentation of the ships, that
> the eyes of the beholders were dazzled, and to those
> looking from afar they seemed of flame rather than of
> wood. For if at any time the sun cast the splendour of its
> rays among them, the flashing of arms shone in one
> place, in another the flame of suspended shields. Gold
> shone on the prows, silver also flashed on the variously
> shaped ships.[xxxiv]

Professor Dodwell discovered that much of what emerges from the study of everyday documents such as wills and charters supports what might otherwise have been taken for artistic hyperbole in poetry:

> If, in *Beowulf,* there are references to a gold-plated hall,
> we are told that, in the eleventh century, the domed
> architectural canopy that surrounded the high altar at
> Waltham was gold plated and had columns, bases and
> arches also embellished with gold, and a tenth-century
> portrayal of another canopy in a cathedral shows parts of
> the capitals and bases in gold. If, in that epic poem, the
> eaves of the same hall were said to be adorned with gold,
> we know that, if life had been his companion, as a

contemporary delicately put it, King Eadred in the tenth
century would have adorned the east porch of the church
at Winchester with gilded tiles. If the same poem
mentions a gold figured tapestry, we know that even
sails in the eleventh century could be embroidered with
historic scenes in gold.[xxxv]

As he points out, the poets were not dreaming up gilded visions
but delineating the tastes of the world around them. The golden
banner that illuminated the dragon's den in *Beowulf* was paralleled
by Harold's golden and jewelled banner of the Fighting Man at
Hastings, sent to the Pope by William after the battle as part of the
spoils of war. Kenneth Clark, in his lectures on civilization, made
the very accurate point that, when an Anglo-Saxon poet wanted
to put his ideal of the good society into words, he spoke of gold.

Particular generosity was lavished on religious books and
codices, and the magnificent standard of their production can be
seen from survivors such as the Lindisfarne Gospels and the
Canterbury Codex Aureus, now in the Stockholm Royal Library.
We know that St Wilfrid commissioned a gospel book for his
church at Ripon in 678, to be 'in letters of purest gold on purpled
parchment and illuminated'; and he had a case made for it of
purest gold, set with gems. Ironically, the very splendour lavished
on such productions was to be their undoing, for it would be the
gold and jewelled covers that attracted the attention of the
illiterate pagan robbers. The Codex Aureus provides an
interesting example of this. It was looted by Vikings who stripped
it of its golden jewelled cover, but had no use for the illuminated
manuscript inside; they therefore sold this back to an Anglo-Saxon
nobleman named Alfred for yet more gold, and it was restored
by him to Canterbury.

Among the interesting characteristics of Anglo-Saxon life noted by Professor Dodwell was the passion for precious possessions in comparison with land which, after the conquest, would be prized by the Normans above any other form of wealth (though this is not to imply that the Anglo-Saxon was indifferent to land; there is ample evidence that he was not). Land, which he could pass on to his heirs, might come later when he could no longer fight; gold came first. It was the responsibility of any lord to reward the warriors who followed him with gold rings and gilded weapons. The aristocratic Anglo-Saxon would have had gold arm-rings (weighing anything up to 100 mancuses of gold at 4 grams a mancus) on both arms, his clothes would have been made of wool and imported silk with woven gold borders, with the addition of furs for warmth; his sword and dagger would have had hilts covered and decorated with gold and silver and inlaid with jewels. He could, in fact, have been wearing the price of a substantial estate. He would retain his warriors by the generosity with which he lavished gold rings and weapons on them. This could (from the point of view of William of Poitiers) be accounted for by a weakness for luxury and display; it was more probably due to the conveniently portable nature of precious metals during periods of invasion and rapine. There is also the point that you could not be taxed on the possession of gold. When Godwin was exiled in 1051, the ample treasury he is reported to have packed into his fleet would have been in gold and jewels. But what Dodwell says of the importance to the Anglo-Saxons of the changing and shifting and reflected light on gold and silver and precious stones in a northern landscape that must for most of the year have been dark and overcast is the most interesting of all:

Æthelwulf remarks on how the changing light gave vibrancy to gold vessels and, in the dark interiors of northern buildings, unlit as yet by a general and generous use of windows, we can understand how the warm glow of gold would give a delicate tremulousness to the surface of art treasures as they caught and reflected at various angles the northern light or the gleam of wax lamps or candles.[xxxvi] . . . Perhaps, indeed, it is in the sea and the mesmeric fascination it still has for us today that we can recapture some of the Anglo-Saxon interest in colour. Though the sea can change almost imperceptibly from blues to bruise-coloured greys and greens, its real visual attraction lies in the fact that each colour can vary within its own range in terms of 'depth' and 'brightness'. The merest ruffling of the surface produces an exciting mobility of brightness of the same hue which gives a new animation and interest to the whole. This vibrancy the Anglo-Saxons managed to achieve even in their coloured outline drawings, and the almost shimmering quality of some of their coloured drawings reminds us of Æthelwulf's interest in the tremulous flames of the hanging torches at night which he likened to gleaming stars.[xxxvii]

Quite apart from its treasures, however, England was, on the whole, a good country to live in by the standards of the times. It was, in many ways, a remarkably fluid society. There were, of course, class distinctions, as there were in every country at that time, but the possibilities of crossing class barriers seem by eleventh-century standards very enlightened. The basic ranks of society under the king, starting from the top, were ealdormen (after Cnut's reign, known as earls), thegns (subdivided into king's thegns, who presumably held land directly from the king, and others who held from intermediate lords, and who roughly equated to gentry and yeomanry), and churls, or free peasants and farmers; these classes were differentiated by their wergild or blood-price, the compensation that had to be paid to their kin if they were killed. The wergild of a nobleman was 1,200 shillings, that of a thegn 600 shillings, that of a churl 200 shillings. Below all these came the unfree men or slaves, who naturally had no wergild. But the situation was not static. A churl who did so well that he possessed five hides of land on which he paid the appropriate taxes was assessed at the wergild of a thegn and achieved a correspondingly higher social status; and if his son and grandson continued to hold the same amount of land, the title, the status and the financial obligations became hereditary. A merchant who had crossed the sea three times in his own ship and at his own risk was also entitled to be upgraded to thegnship, a significant encouragement to trade. An unfree man could be manumitted by his lord and become free and technically could start to aim at thegnship. Equally in times of hardship and famine, a man might, in desperation, sell himself or his family into slavery for the sake of food and maintenance, and a free man who failed or was unable to pay judicial fines might be sentenced to lose his liberty and become unfree. If he were, he could be redeemed by his relatives on payment of a stipulated sum. It was a system where, by contrast with Normandy, less attention was paid to blood or descent than to achievement. Earl Godwin, the most powerful man in England under the king, was the grandson of a Sussex thegn of no particular distinction. Society in Anglo-Saxon England was, as in contemporary Europe, brutal, violent and frequently unjust; but there were more aspects of it that mitigated the general misery than elsewhere.

Many of the ideas relating to family were remarkably modern. The position of women in society might well have been envied by their descendants in the post-conquest period and much later; it is clearly stated in the law-codes that 'no woman or maiden shall ever be forced to marry one whom she dislikes, nor be sold for money'. She had legal rights to shares in the property of the household and to the care of the children if there were a divorce or separation and, if widowed, a second marriage was, in theory at least, entirely at her own discretion. Indeed, according to the first Kentish laws, divorce was extremely easy in Anglo-Saxon society; a woman who wished to leave her marriage with her children was entitled to half the goods of the household. Her freedom to own and dispose of land was remarkable, compared with the post-conquest period when the property of a woman became the property of her husband the moment she married. It has been suggested that Harold's mistress or handfasted wife, Edith,[xxxviii] may have been the woman named in the Domesday Book as Edith the Fair or Edith the Rich, in which case she clearly came of good family and held extensive lands in her own right throughout East Anglia and Buckinghamshire. The Domesday Book also records the situation of a woman in Yorkshire called Asa who held her land

> separate and free from the rule and control of
> Beornwulf, her husband, even when they were together,
> in such a way that he himself could make neither gift
> nor sale of it, nor forfeit it. After their separation she
> herself withdrew with all her land and possessed it as its
> lady.[xxxix]

Not until the passing of the Married Women's Property Act in 1882 were women to enjoy such financial independence again.

Moreover, a woman did not have to be of noble birth to enjoy such rights: the Domesday Book records the grant to Ælfgyth the maid of two hides of land in Buckinghamshire

> which she could give or sell to whom she wished, and of the demesne farm of King Edward she herself had half a hide which Godric the sheriff granted her as long as he was sheriff, on condition of her teaching his daughter gold embroidery work.[xl]

Gold embroidery work was, of course, one of the most highly prized and rewarded skills of the time and one for which the English were particularly renowned.

As for the upbringing of children, the ideas expressed in one of the gnomic poems (essentially collections of sententious utterances) were positively advanced even by twentieth-century standards:

> One shall not rebuke a youth in his childhood, until he can reveal himself. He shall thrive among the people in that he is confident.

The history of education in Anglo-Saxon England divides into five periods: the conversion period, when missionaries from both Rome and Ireland brought learning and books with them; the first high period of the Church, when Alcuin, an English missionary at the court of Charlemagne, recalled regretfully the richness of the library of York Minster that he had left behind and of which Alfred was thinking when he remembered the churches filled with treasures and books; the first Danish invasions, in which so many of those books and treasures were plundered or destroyed; the beginning of the revival of learning under Alfred, and the gradual building up again of libraries and teachers during the peaceful times of Athelstan and Edgar; and then the second wave of Viking invasions under Æthelred, less destructive than the first but bad enough. At least Cnut was a devout Christian and his father Sweyn Forkbeard nominally one – Æthelred never had to answer the unanswerable question his forefather Alfred was faced with: how can you trust the oaths of pagans to whom nothing is sacred, not even their own gods?

The first and most important educational necessity throughout these centuries was to train recruits for the priesthood and the cloister. That the various minster schools succeeded in this is indicated by the number of English missionaries who went to convert the heathen on the Continent, such as St Boniface, or were sent for to take education and civilization to foreign schools, as Alcuin was recruited by Charlemagne. These men were accustomed to send back to England for books unavailable to them where they were working; English book production was clearly of a high standard. Boniface wrote to ask the Abbess Eadburh to copy St Peter's epistles for him in gold. This would presumably be for ceremonial occasions, but more workaday books were in demand also. Dorothy Whitelock listed the writings that were then available in England:

> They were, of course, familiar with the Bible and the
> writings of the Christian Fathers, and with the Christian
> poets, Juvencus, Prudentius, Sedulius, Prosper,
> Fortunatus, Lactantius, and Arator. Bede makes use of a
> number of historical writings, of Josephus, Eusebius (in
> Latin translation from the Greek), Orosius, Cassiodorus,
> Gregory of Tours, etc., and of saints' lives such as

Paulinus's *Life of Ambrose*, Possidius's *Life of Augustine,* Constantius's *Life of Germanus*. Of classical authors, both Bede and Aldhelm knew Virgil and Pliny at first hand, and Aldhelm used Lucan, Ovid, Cicero, and Sallust. Citations of other authors occur, but could have been taken from the works of Isidore of Seville, or from the Latin grammarians, of whom a really remarkable number were available in England already in the seventh century. Some very rare works had already found their way to England, and one, the grammar of Julian of Toledo, owes its preservation to this circumstance, for all surviving manuscripts go back to an English copy.[xli]

And the English monastics were not just reading these books, they were writing new works for themselves. Bede's and Aldhelm's works were produced at this period.

It is impossible to know how far learning reached the lay population in the eighth and ninth centuries. There may have been, probably were, noblemen and women who were literate and could read Latin as well as English. Many of the most famous founders of monasteries, such as Benedict Biscop, the founder of Bede's monastery of Jarrow/Monkwearmouth, and a noted buyer of books, must have come into this category; many, like him, must have entered monasteries or taken holy orders later in life. If there had been no tradition at all of lay education, Alfred would hardly have lamented in his letter on the state of learning in England (?890s) that there were now few people north or south of the Humber who could even read English or translate a letter from Latin into English, or make use of the books that remained. It is not entirely clear from his letter whether he is thinking of clerics or laypeople or both. He may have been thinking primarily of priests or monks; but if he had been thinking only of the clergy, his programme of translations into English of the books that were most necessary for *all* men to know would look rather strange. He would never have supposed that it would have been sufficient for a priest or a monk to know only these particular books and only in English. Their needs would have been far more extensive. His programme of translation, as well as his own words, 'all men', imply a determination to reach the laity. Asser, one of the scholars whom Alfred recruited to make his court a centre of learning, speaks in his life of Alfred of the king's children being educated

> in company with all the nobly born children of virtually
> the entire area, and a good many of lesser birth as well.
> In this school, books in both languages – that is to say, in
> Latin and English – were carefully read; they also
> devoted themselves to writing, to such an extent that,
> even before they had the requisite strength for manly
> skills (hunting, that is, and other skills appropriate to
> noblemen), they were seen to be devoted and intelligent
> students of the liberal arts.[xlii]

We may well suspect that Asser is laying it on a little lavishly here, but even allowing for exaggeration, his specific mention of other noble children and some of lesser birth makes it fairly clear that, in theory at least, Alfred's conception of education was not limited to the Church and that the origins of comprehensive education may be found in England nearly two hundred years before the conquest.

There is no such direct testimony of the state of general literacy as Alfred provides in his letter from the reigns of his immediate successors, but there is little doubt that many could and did read. Professor James Campbell comments:

> The use of written English went with a considerable degree of lay literacy; no doubt as both cause and effect. Æthelweard's translation of the Chronicle was the first book written by an English nobleman and, for nearly four centuries, the last. Two of Ælfric's theological treatises were written for thegns. The relative abundance of inscriptions, not only on churches but also on, for example, brooches and rings, is suggestive. A layman who learned to read in the Confessor's reign would be able to make out his father's will, the king's writs, the boundary clause of a charter, or a monastery's inventories. In Henry II's day, mere literacy would have won him none of these advantages. If he wanted them he had to learn Latin. There is no doubt that some did so; but it would be unwise to be confident that they were more numerous than those who were literate in English a century or more earlier. If the late Anglo-Saxon state was run with sophistication and thoughtfulness, this may very well be connected with the ability of many laymen to read.[xliii]

In addition to these legally useful documents, the religious texts available to the Anglo-Saxon layman in English would have included the Gospels, the psalms, the Hexateuch, the creed, the confessional formulae, homilies and the lives of the saints. Ælfric's translation into English of the Old Testament was commissioned by a nobleman. Perhaps he wanted to have it read to him in his own tongue; but possibly he wanted to be able to read it himself.

It is worth remembering that, from the earliest period, the various codes of laws had all been written in English, implying an ability in those who were not Latinists to read them. After a papal council at Rheims in 1050, King Edward ordered that a record of what had been said and done there should be written in English and a copy kept in the king's treasury. This would not be necessary for the clergy and could therefore only have been designed for the convenience of laymen. There is a tradition that King Harold owned books – not just religious books, which any pious man might have, but books on hawking – which has caused his biographer to hazard the cautious guess that he may have been literate. It would be more surprising if he had not been. He had been virtually running the highly sophisticated Anglo-Saxon state of which Professor Campbell speaks for years before he was crowned; a state in which, since at least the days of Alfred, one of the primary instruments of government was the royal writ, which recipients were expected to be able to read. His sister, the queen, had received an excellent education at the abbey of Wilton, where there was a school for aristocratic young ladies, and one may assume that her younger sister, Gunnhild, who later took the veil, had been similarly educated; it would be strange if less trouble had been taken over the education of the boys of the family. We know from the anonymous author of the *Vita Ædwardi* that Godwin took care to have his sons trained in all the accomplishments that would make them useful to their king. Indeed, Frank Barlow has pointed out that, of all the English kings after Cnut, Harold was the only one who received a political education suitable for the office.[xliv] There is no evidence either way for Duke William's literacy. One of his biographers asserts categorically that he was not and that all his sons were similarly illiterate.[xlv] The Norman court, he points out, was not a centre of culture. Orderic

Vitalis writes of his having witnessed a charter by making a cross.[xlvi] Indeed, the point has been made by David Bates that, 'for almost the first century of its existence, the government of the Norman rulers was illiterate'[xlvii] – a circumstance that considerably complicates the writing of its history during that period. After Hastings, the new regime was to be much distressed to discover the extent to which English was used for the everyday affairs of church and state; the Normans made haste to substitute Latin, which their own clerks were able to understand.

Alongside the literacy or otherwise of the laity in England was something that is much more easily estimated: their affection for the old Germanic heroic poems and lays. This was one of the most lasting gifts that they brought from their continental homelands and it endured right up to the conquest. Of all the countries of Europe at that time, England was far ahead in having a flourishing vernacular literature, much of which is unfortunately lost, though enough has survived to give us a feeling for its quality. Before 1066, there was little to challenge it, apart from the Celtic literature of Ireland and Wales and the French *chansons de geste,* the stories of heroic deeds, of which there were probably once many, though few, and those mostly considerably later, have survived. The *Chanson de Roland* is the most important early example to survive and cannot much pre-date the conquest in its present form. There had certainly been vernacular poetry on heroic subjects in Germany, but it was mainly oral; only scraps and shards of this have survived in written form, such as the tantalizingly short piece of the heroic poem *Hildebrand.* The great age of the Icelandic sagas came well after the conquest.

England, on the other hand, had the distinction of having poems not just of heroic deeds but also of a more reflective nature, asking the questions that good poetry has always asked about the unfathomable mystery of existence. It is miraculous that we have as much of it as we do: the odds must always have been heavily against its survival. In its original form, when the Anglo-Saxons first came to England, it must have been a purely oral tradition that they brought with them. When a more literate age arrived with the conversion, it was highly unlikely that the monks, then the only literate people, would have given priority to committing the pagan songs of pagan gods and heroes to paper. (Though it is a mistake to exaggerate the prudishness of the cloister; Professor Campbell has pointed out that a tenth-century transcription of Ovid's *Ars Amatoria,* the part concerned with the techniques of seduction, may well be in the hand of St Dunstan.) But the songs did somehow survive, indeed they must have flourished, and even in monasteries they must have had a following, or Alcuin would not have asked the Abbot of Lindisfarne his indignant question, *Quid enim Hinieldus cum Christo?,* 'What has Ingeld to do with Christ?' Ingeld, prince of the Heathobards, makes a brief appearance in *Beowulf,* the only surviving Anglo-Saxon epic, in one of its many digressions through old Germanic legend. Freawaru, daughter of Hrothgar, the King of the Danes, is given to him in marriage to heal the breach between his people and hers. But, prophesies Beowulf, the peace offering will surely turn sour, when the Heathobards see the daughter of their enemy at the feast, and indeed the blood feud breaks out again even more strongly with Ingeld torn between love for his bride and his duty of revenge and loyalty to his people. The fact that he could be referred to so allusively, both in *Beowulf* and in Alcuin's letter, implies the existence at some time of many well-known songs or poems about Ingeld and the Danish/Heathobard feud, so that the hearers or readers of *Beowulf* would quickly pick up the allusion.

There is a similar reference in *Beowulf* to the story of a fight at Finnesburg, of which we have confirmation in a mere fifty lines of another poem on the subject; the fragment of vellum on which it was originally written has vanished since it was transcribed in the seventeenth century but, to judge by what we have, it must have been a poem of considerable distinction, though probably shorter than *Beowulf*. The fragment describes the resumption of another blood feud; the young prince, trapped in the hall of his host, sees lights in the night sky and warns his followers that they signal the advance of enemies:

> Here there is no dawn from the east, here no dragons fly,
> It is not the horns of this hall that burn,
> They come to attack us. Birds sing,
> The grey wolf howls, wooden war-gear echoes,
> Shields receive the spear. Now shines the moon,
> Wandering beneath the clouds; now arise deeds of woe
> That will work harm to our people.

It is the combination of the small natural details (the alarmed birds singing, the moon shining erratically through the clouds) with the more standard descriptions of heroic lays (the wolf howling, the sound of spear on shield) that gives it its peculiarly evocative magic. But what is common to all the surviving Anglo-Saxon heroic poetry – *Beowulf,* the remains of *Finnesburh* and *Waldere,* the remnant of a poem on Walther of Aquitaine (and also in the remnant we have of the Old High German *Hildebrand*) – is a dignity of proportion and style that gives it its indubitably epic stature. Beowulf being received by Hrothgar at Heorot is fully comparable to Odysseus at the court of Alcinous. Heroic epic rarely springs, fully formed, from the head of an original poet;

generations of shorter, possibly cruder lays and songs on its subject herald its appearance. Many generations of legends and shorter poems on the subject of Beowulf and his exploits, now lost, must have preceded and generated the epic we have now. Not all would have been in English, but some undoubtedly were.

Beowulf itself (probably dating from the eighth century in its present form) has only survived through a series of happy accidents, the last being the rescue in 1731 of the only surviving manuscript (though in a damaged form) from the disastrous fire in the Cottonian Library in Ashburnham House, Westminster, in which it was then held. As with so much else of the civilization of the Anglo-Saxons, we are tormented by our ignorance of what has been lost, as well as grateful for the little that has been saved. Not all of what has endured is on the epic scale or concerns blood feuds and monsters. Among the rest is something that at that date was peculiar to England – as far as we know, that is, since again we can never know what has been lost of the work of other countries – and that is poetry of a more reflective nature. Most of it has a peculiarly elegiac or lyrical character. Some are shorter poems reflecting on the human condition, the loss of a lord, a wife deserted by her husband, a husband who has made good overseas sending for his wife. Many mourn the transitory nature of worldly happiness, such as *The Ruin,* in which the poet broods over the remains of what was probably an ancient Roman city, possibly Bath, or *The Wanderer* in which the narrator laments:

> A wise man may grasp how ghastly it shall be
> When all this world's wealth standeth waste
> Even as now, in many places over the earth,
> Walls stand, wind beaten,

Heavy with hoar frost; ruined habitations. . .
The maker of men has so marred this dwelling
That human laughter is not heard about it
And idle stand these old giant works.

How that time is gone, he mourns, vanished beneath the shadow
of night, as though it had never been. But if the predominant
mood of Anglo-Saxon poetry was elegiac, it was flexible enough
to serve other purposes: to depict the frenzy of battle, as when the
sparks from the clashing swords blaze 'as if all Finnesburh were
aflame' or to portray the almost Miltonic ambition and resentment
of Satan in the retelling of the Genesis story ('I could be God as
well as He'). The Old English *Genesis* may have been a biblical
story, but Satan, declaring war on heaven, does so in the old
Germanic heroic spirit:

Strong comrades, bold-hearted heroes, stand by me, who
will not fail me in the fight; they, brave men, have
chosen me for their master. With such can a man lay a
plan, carry it out with such companions in war. They are
keen in their friendship to me, loyal in their hearts; I can
be their leader, rule in this kingdom. Thus it seems not
right to me that I need flatter God any whit for any
benefit; no longer will I be his follower.[xlviii]

But he finds himself in another land, 'void of light and teeming
with flame, a great peril of fire', many hundreds of years before
Milton described a later Satan's 'darkness visible'.

There are quantities of riddles, a verse form in which even
monks thought it permissible to indulge (which is presumably
why so many, comparatively speaking, have survived) and which

frequently illuminates life in Anglo-Saxon England. This riddle has more modern resonances:

> The monster came sailing, wondrous along the wave; it
> called out in its comeliness to the land from the ship;
> loud was its din; its laughter was terrible, dreadful on
> earth; its edges were sharp. It was malignantly cruel, not
> easily brought to battle but fierce in the fighting; it stove
> in the ship's sides, relentless and ravaging. It bound it
> with a baleful charm; it spoke with cunning of its own
> nature: 'My mother is of the dearest race of maidens, she
> is my daughter grown to greatness, as it is known to
> men, to people among the fold, that she shall stand with
> joy on the earth in all lands.'[xlix]

It is an iceberg.

And there is that unforgettable, extraordinarily powerful and fully achieved masterpiece, *The Dream of the Rood,* in which Christ's cross speaks of its experience of the crucifixion with a passion and imaginative originality that were not to be recaptured in English poetry for three centuries after the conquest:

> As a rood was I raised up; I bore aloft the mighty King,
> the Lord of Heaven; I durst not stoop. They pierced me
> with dark nails; the wounds are still plain to view in me,
> gaping gashes of malice; I durst not do hurt to any of
> them. They bemocked us together. I was all bedewed
> with blood, shed from the Man's side, after He had sent
> forth His Spirit. I have endured many stern trials on the
> hill; I saw the God of hosts violently stretched out;
> darkness with its clouds had covered the Lord's corpse,

the fair radiance; a shadow went forth, dark beneath the
clouds. All creation wept, lamented the King's death;
Christ was on the cross.[1]

When poetry was written in English again, it had a different
character, the difference not always easy to define but probably
due in part to the fact that, while before the conquest much of the
most impressive work had been written for an aristocratic
audience or readership, by the time of its revival it was being
written for a more popular and provincial public. It was not until
the fourteenth century that it regained its old authority.

Anglo-Saxon poetry has been accused of a gloomy over-
emphasis on the darker side of human existence. It is true that it
tends to dwell on the transitoriness of life and of pleasure;
happiness in any Dark Age society probably was transitory. But
it reflects the circumstances of the life in which it was written.
Just as the Anglo-Saxons' love of gold was derived in part from
the way its radiance lighted the darkness and cold of their
churches and houses, so their poetry mirrors the harshness of their
daily existence. The reader is always conscious of the gloom and
wildness of the northern landscape that produced it: the cold, the
hard life extracting a living from the soil, the seaspray in the face,
the loneliness of a life deprived of the support of a lord, contrasted
with the warmth and joy of feasting in the hall and the company
of comrades. It calls to mind Bede's famous story of the
Northumbrian ealdorman's comparison of the life of man to the
sparrow flying through the warm lighted hall, passing from the
cold darkness outside to another unknown darkness on the other
side. There is none of the joy of the merry month of May in Anglo-
Saxon poetry. But there is a noble melancholy and an elegiac
lyricism, combined with a stoic acceptance of fate, and a courage

'perfect, because without hope',[li] exquisitely summed up in the words of Byrhtwold, the old retainer, at the battle of Maldon:

> Mind shall be the braver, heart be the fiercer,
> Courage be the greater, as our strength lessens.
> Here lies our lord, hacked and cut down,
> A brave man in the dust; ever will he mourn
> Who thinks from this war-play to return home.

England was unique in Europe in 1066 in having a fully developed vernacular prose. Its most remarkable manifestation is, of course, the Anglo-Saxon Chronicle, which recorded in English events from the seventh century onwards at a time when chronicles would normally have been written in Latin. It was, in fact, not one chronicle but several, different versions being maintained at different ecclesiastical centres around the country. Its establishment has been credited to Alfred, as part of his campaign to promote writing in English that could be read in their own tongue by all of his people who were literate. There is no written evidence to support the claim, but the coincidence of the appearance of a chronicle in English at the time when Alfred was campaigning for essential books to be available in English is, to say the least, suggestive, especially since it would have taken a certain amount of central authority to get the project going in the first place. Whatever the origin of the Chronicle, it does, in itself, provide an overview of the development of written English, from the earliest entries, such as the rather incoherent but vivid account of the blood feud in 755 between Cynewulf and Cyneheard (the first ever substantial piece of historical writing in Europe in any vernacular) to the bitter irony of the late tenth- and early eleventh-century entries on the Danish raids in the reign of Æthelred and the fluency and power of the account of Count Eustace's affray at Dover and the outlawing of the Godwin family in 1051. The Cynewulf and Cyneheard episode gives a fair sample of Alfredian prose in its early stages, though it may be a reworking of an earlier account of the episode that had been handed down: after telling us that Cynewulf had held the kingdom of the West Saxons for thirty-one winters, it continues:

> He wished to drive out a prince named Cyneheard. . .
> and when [Cyneheard] heard that the king was lying
> with a woman at Merton, he rode there and surrounded
> the bower before the king's men were aware of him.
> And when the king perceived that, he went to the door
> and there valiantly defended himself until he saw the
> prince and then rushed at him and severely wounded
> him. And then they were all fighting with the king until
> they had slain him. And when the king's men heard the
> din from the woman's bower they rushed there, whoever
> was readiest and swiftest; and the prince offered all of
> them life and goods but none would accept. And they
> fought together until all were slain but one Welsh
> hostage, and he was badly wounded. And in the
> morning when the king's thegns that had been left
> behind heard that the king was dead they rode thither
> with his ealdorman Osric and his thegn Wiferth and the
> men who had been left behind, and found the prince
> where the king lay slain and the gates had been locked
> against them, and there they were fighting. And he
> offered them lands and goods at their own choice if they
> would grant him the kingdom, and told them that
> kinsmen of theirs were within who would not go from

him. And they answered that no kinsmen were dearer to them than their lord, and they would never follow his slayer. And they offered that their kinsmen should go safely hence; and they said that the same had been offered to their companions who had been with the king. They said that they cared for this 'no more than your companions who were slain with the king'. And they were fighting around the gates until they got inside and slew the prince and all who were with him, all but one who was the ealdorman's godson, and his life was spared though he was much wounded.

The confusion of personal pronouns, the abrupt unexplained switch from the third to the second person, all mark it out as early experimental prose; but nothing conceals the vitality and immediacy of the account given, even though it must have been written well over a hundred years after the events described. The contrast in fluency and control with the much later Chronicle extracts already quoted is striking but this early piece was written by a clerk who already had an instinctive feeling for the rhythms and potentialities of English prose.

Outside the Chronicle, it is equally possible to track the development of the language in flexibility and sophistication from the slightly elementary individuality and sincerity of Alfred's first efforts to the fiery eloquence of Archbishop Wulfstan's *Sermon of the Wolf* and the classic elegance of Ælfric. It is impossible not to wonder what would have resulted if the language had been allowed to continue along its well-established trajectory; but the development of the prose, like that of the poetry, was stamped out brutally overnight on 14 October 1066. When in the 1070s the English language ceased to be used for political and administrative purposes, there was no longer any central authority to establish and propagate a standard 'received' English and it broke down into a confusion of regional dialects. Indeed, it is likely that the written Old English that has descended to us, the Wessex form of the language, must always have been something of a literary and bureaucratic mandarin, probably different from its spoken form even in Wessex, certainly different from what was spoken in Mercia or Northumbria. With the loss of its dominance, the regional variants had their way. Thus, when English prose began to be used again for literary purposes, three centuries later, it was, in effect, a new English, and had returned to the tentative experimentalism that Old English had shown in Alfred's day. Not until Malory's *Morte d'Arthur,* roughly four hundred years after the conquest, did it show itself again as a fully developed literary medium.

THE ARMIES

The predominating ethos of Dark Age societies was martial; the king functioned first and foremost as a war-leader and as the defender of his people, and the more effective he was in this capacity, the higher his standing with his own people and his enemies. It was King Alfred who, in his translation of Boethius' *Consolation of Philosophy*, first defined what he called the tools of his kingship by separating them into what would be the traditional three classes, the praying men, the fighting men and the working men; but there was never any doubt about which of them formed the aristocracy. In England, as in Normandy, the ability to fight was the most important qualification for life, and the reputation of a renowned warrior the most eagerly sought.

It may seem rather contradictory, therefore, to make the point that major pitched battles, like Hastings, were on the whole avoided whenever possible, and the most successful rulers of the day were generally those who were most efficient in avoiding them. It has been pointed out that the only major battlefield on which William had appeared before Hastings was that of Val-ès-Dunes, when he was only nineteen and where the commander-in-chief was his overlord, the King of France. Over the next twenty years until Hastings, he contrived with considerable adroitness to achieve his objectives by more indirect methods such as siege-work, in which in his early years at least he appears to have been masterly. The battle of Mortemer, in which the Normans defeated the French under the French king and the Count of Anjou, was captained on the Norman side by William's cousin, Robert of Eu, and the battle of Varaville against the same opponents, where William managed to catch the French army divided in two on either side of a ford, indicates patience and clever tactics but can hardly be compared with a battle of the scale of Hastings. Harold, in his warfare against the Welsh king Gruffydd ap Llewellyn in 1062, showed something of the same tendency. He pursued an extremely effective campaign of harassment against him, but the hands that eventually killed Gruffydd were Welsh, not English. On the whole he appears to have preferred negotiation to battle and to have resorted to force only when diplomacy failed. Edward, on the other hand, despite his saintly reputation, seems to have favoured warfare rather than diplomacy on the occasions for which we have evidence (for example, the exiling of the Godwin family in 1051 and the Northumbrian rebellion in 1065): a not uncommon example of the civilian who knew little at first hand of war contrasted with the soldier who knew all too much about it.

The reason is not difficult to find. Far too much must be hazarded on the outcome of a single pitched battle, and, unless the odds on one side were overwhelming (in which case the lesser side would if it could find a way to avoid battle, such as retreating), the eventual outcome was far too uncertain for the hazard to be worthwhile. The principle was summed up succinctly by Vegetius in his *De Re Militari*, the military bible of the Middle Ages, probably written about AD 390: battle should be the last resort, everything else should be tried first. 'The main and principal point in war,' he went on, 'is to secure plenty of provisions for oneself and to destroy the enemy by famine. Famine is more terrible than the sword.'[lii] The tactic of harrying and devastating the enemy's territory (as Harold did in Wales and as William did when he landed in England) had the double advantage of damaging the enemy's prestige and economy, and maintaining the invading army at no cost to the invader. As has been pointed out, one man's foraging is another man's ravaging. It was also a procedure much more popular with the individual soldier. In ravaging (or foraging), he not only looked after his own commissariat, he also had the chance of plunder. In battle, he was much more likely to be killed. It has been suggested that the harrying of Harold's lands in Wessex was the most effective stratagem used by William to provoke Harold into confronting him at the earliest possible opportunity. And it was, of course, what the Viking raiders did in the ninth and tenth centuries. Apart from the five pitched battles of Edmund Ironside against Cnut and, of course, the battle of Maldon, there had been few major battles against the Vikings since Alfred's conclusive victory at Edington. It follows that over the century before Hastings, the English defence capability had been geared more to combat guerrilla Viking invasions than to battles on the Stamford Bridge or Hastings scale, the one notable exception being Athelstan's great victory in 937 at the battle of Brunanburh over the combined forces of the kings of Scotland and Ireland.

The myth of an Anglo-Saxon army primarily made up of peasants fighting with sticks and stones was exploded many years ago but dies very hard. Such an army could not have held back the Normans for half an hour, let alone a full day. Another myth, strenuously promoted in some circles in recent years, is that the victory of the Normans was that of a highly disciplined feudal force, composed in large part of well-trained cavalry, over some kind of home guard fighting on foot, enthusiastic but poorly equipped and largely untrained, called together in haste from the shires to meet the threat of invasion but hampered by obsolete organization in the face of the sophisticated opposition. In part, this is due to the retrospective effect of the outcome: the English army was defeated by the Norman army, therefore it must, *ipso facto,* have been inferior. This argument does not take account of the circumstances in which the battle was fought.

A good deal of research has been done on the composition of the two armies that met at Hastings, but in essentials there are several unknowable facts, the most important of which is our ignorance of the size of the two forces. Many efforts have been made to compute these, on the one side from the numbers of men and horses whose heads are shown above the gunwales in the Norman ships in the Bayeux Tapestry (and the belief that one can extrapolate from this a calculation based on the number of ships believed to have sailed), on the other on the assumed length of the English position and the probable depth of Harold's deployment along it. Neither hypothesis can provide a reliable result. The depictions on the Tapestry are symbolic, not naturalistic, and we have no detailed knowledge of the types or sizes of the ships William built; and the topography of Harold's original position has been changed so much by time and building work that it cannot support any reliable calculation. There is also the unreliability of the contemporary evidence. On the English side, the Anglo-Saxon Chronicle, corroborated by some later chroniclers, states that Harold fought before many of his troops had come up – contradicted by a different assertion, that in fact he had too many men for the position he occupied. On the Norman side, there are wildly unrealistic estimates of the size of the English army, designed in part, probably, to enhance the duke's prestige in having beaten so colossal a force. As for the Norman army, William announced before the battle that if he had only 10,000 men rather than the 60,000 he had brought he would still fight Harold, but this was undoubtedly a rhetorical figure and 60,000 is not credible. The possibility of armies of 20,000 or more on each side has been suggested, but is unlikely. The best guesses of the best authorities, based on calculations of the size of the battlefield, the number of men it could accommodate and the space between them that would be necessary for them to fight effectively, are that the two armies were fairly evenly matched, at between 6,000 and 8,000 men on each side, and this is borne out by the length of the battle since one would not expect a battle where one side was demonstrably superior to the other to last so long. But they are no more than guesses.

Ironically, of the two forces we know far more about the obsolete English than the professional Norman, and what can be deduced from the written evidence available does not support the idea of an out-of-date amateur force, crushed by a highly trained professional army organized along feudal lines. This is not surprising, given the length of time over which the English system had evolved and the various Viking invasions to which it had been forced to react. There must always, from the earliest days and on both sides of the Channel, have been some arrangements, of varying degrees of formality, linking the defence of a country to the holding of land in that country, so that all free landholders had a responsibility to the king, or to some intermediary lord, to give armed service when required. Vestiges of such a system over the previous centuries can be found in many parts of Europe. England, by coincidence, provides more evidence of its development than Normandy.

Long before the advent of the Vikings, the rulers of the individual kingdoms of the Heptarchy had had occasion to call on their subjects for fighting men. It was as a result of the ninth-century raids that Alfred made the most far-reaching changes yet to the organization of that requirement. It was he who initiated the systematized construction of fortified towns or *burhs* (or boroughs, as they became) throughout his kingdom, to be permanently maintained in a state of readiness and defence; in theory no one was more than twenty miles away from a place of refuge in the event of Viking attack. The germ of this idea had been found earlier in Mercia, but it was Alfred who saw its relevance to the kind of hit and run raids to which so many parts of England had been subjected, though it was left to his son, Edward the Elder, to complete the scheme. Edward also produced the complicated Burghal Hidage document, which provided for the maintenance and defence of the *burhs* and has been described as a watershed in the history of Anglo-Saxon governance.[liii] The lack of castles in England has been seen as a sign of the general backwardness of the English in military matters, in comparison with the achievements of the castle-building Normans, and Orderic Vitalis ascribes the speed with which William was able to subdue the country after Hastings to the absence of English castles. But the virtue of castles lay chiefly in the part they could play in defending border territory (most of the few English castles that existed before 1066 were on the Welsh marches), or in holding down rebellious or conquered territory (the reason why William built so many of them) or in providing a focus for insurrection. In the centuries after the conquest, the many English castles held by rebellious nobles were to prove a mixed blessing to William's successors. Alfred's system of fortified *burhs* whose administration and upkeep were in the hands of their inhabitants, not of individual nobles, and into which country-dwellers could retreat for safety in time of danger represented a much nobler vision and proved an effective deterrent to Viking raiders.

It was Alfred, too, who solved the problem of raiders who could attack and disperse before the English shire levies could be called out; he arranged a rota, as described in the Anglo-Saxon Chronicle, so that half the fighting force would always be on military duty while the other half remained at home for purposes of immediate local defence and maintaining the general affairs of the country. This produced what was, in effect, the first English standing army, and it worked. But in order for it to work, he had to tighten up the legislation that laid the duty on the land to produce the fighting men he needed. It is also Alfred who is credited with laying the foundations of the English navy when in 897 he commissioned the building of a fleet of longships to his own design, though in action these proved less successful than his other innovations, being too deep in the draught for the river work in which the shallower Viking ships excelled. None the less, his was the first recorded attempt to construct an official naval force for the defence of the nation, and his successors were to build on his achievements.

Naturally, there had been many changes in the detailed organization of the national defence between Alfred's death in 899 and the mid-eleventh century. During the more peaceful years of the tenth century, the upkeep and manning of the *burhs* was not maintained with the same rigour as had originally been intended, and it was no longer necessary to keep a standing army in the field. As time went on, though the service due from landowners was strictly maintained, there was a move to allowing it to be commuted for a cash payment with which paid troops could be hired. The Danegeld or heregeld, in the reign of

Æthelred, was not used exclusively for paying the Danes to go away; it often paid one lot of Danish troops to fight off another, as Æthelred paid the famous Viking Thorkell the Tall for many years. After Cnut's introduction of the housecarls in 1018, and their development into the front-line troops of the English army, cash was needed to pay them. But the theoretical obligation of all free men to give military service remained, and could be and was called on. There were clearly enormous variations in detail in different parts of the country, but in general there seem to have been two different types of service: first, the system by which the king could call on a force of warriors for a particular purpose, based on the provision of a man for a certain unit of land; second, the responsibility of all free men to defend the country in an emergency such as an invasion. In the first case, the man was provided, armed, paid and provisioned by the lord, the abbey, the village, the hundred from which he was due, and was expected to serve anywhere needed, at home or abroad, for a certain period, usually sixty days. These would be the men who were normally referred to as the shire levies or the select fyrd. In the second, when all free men were expected to turn out for a national emergency, they were not normally expected to go beyond their own locality and had to be able to return to their own homes at night (there were exceptions on the Scottish and Welsh marches); this has been described as the general fyrd. When Byrhtnoth called together his force to meet the Danes at Maldon, he would have called out the shire levies and his own retainers, but he would almost certainly have regarded this as the sort of emergency in which all the local free men should come to the national defence. This might account for the presence of Dunhere, the 'unorne ceorl', the simple peasant, though he might just as easily have been there as part of the shire levies.

The provision of men for the shire levies was the most important part of the defensive system and was related to the tenure of land. The general basis (allowing for regional differences, for example in the Danelaw where the land was assessed in carucates, not hides) is set out fairly clearly in the account of Wallingford in the Domesday Book, and it was probably in accordance with this system that the summons would have been sent out in 1066:

> If the king sent out an army anywhere only 1 thegn went out from 5 hides, and for his sustenance or pay 4s. for 2 months was given him from each hide. This money, however, was not sent to the king but given to the thegns. If anyone summoned on military service did not go he forfeited all his land to the king.[liv]

If the landowner went himself, he presumably paid himself from the profits of his land; if a man who was not a landholder (or held a unit of less than five hides) went, he would collect his pay or the balance of it from those who did own the land that he was representing. But there are indications throughout the Domesday Book that it was usually the same man who answered the call on any individual territory unless he was unavoidably prevented (perhaps by increasing age or by sickness), and that he went well armed and equipped, suggesting that he was a reasonably experienced fighter. The evidence of the Domesday Book indicates that in 1066 the summons was to the general fyrd, since it gives instances where more than one man had gone to the army for less than five hides; and in this case they cannot all have been able to return to their homes at night.

There is also evidence that in general, representatives from the same shire tended to fight together, and thus would have become accustomed to operating as a trained unit. Throughout the Chronicle there are reports that the men of this shire turned out on this occasion or the men of that shire repelled a landing on another or that an ealdorman opposed an enemy with the levies of such and such shires. Legend has it, for example, that the men of Kent traditionally had the honour of forming the vanguard in any campaign in which they fought and striking the first blow in any battle; the men of London traditionally fought around the king. It is tempting to see in these early arrangements the origins of the county regiments that mostly survived until the late twentieth century and were such a distinguished part of English military history. It was, on the whole, a remarkably efficient and sophisticated system. It could be abused, though there is little evidence that it was in pre-conquest days; the worst example is that of William Rufus who in 1094 summoned an army of 20,000 men and marched them to the coast where he demanded that each man gave him 10s. they were carrying out of the 20s. that they were due (they would have received the balance when they returned home), and then sent them home again, thus raising the enormous sum of £10,000. This is recorded by several chroniclers. The story does nothing for William Rufus's reputation but it does indicate that if that number of men had set out each with the same sum of money, there must have been a fairly uniform system in operation and that it had outlasted the conquest. There is no reason to see why it should have produced a less efficient or well-trained force than any other. It has been well described by C. Warren Hollister:

> The personnel of the select fyrd was heterogeneous
> because the obligation was based upon units of land

rather than social rank. Throughout much of England, each five-hide unit was obliged to produce a warrior-representative. The *miles* who was produced was normally a thegn, but if no thegns were available he might be a man of lower status. He might be a member of one of the intermediate groups – a *cniht,* a *radmannus,* a sokeman. And he might, if necessary, be a well-armed and well-supported member of the ordinary peasantry. The important thing was that he represented an appreciable territorial unit which was obliged to give him generous financial support. As such, he belonged to an exclusive military group which can, in a sense, be considered a class in itself. And he may well have taken considerable pride in his connection with the select territorial army of Saxon England.[lv]

There is no reason to suppose that the shire levies were any less well equipped than the Norman infantry they would have encountered at Hastings. There is plenty of evidence that those who served were expected to present themselves with body armour and appropriate weapons. Perhaps the best evidence of this is found in the heriot or tax that was payable on the death of a thegn to his lord; this was, in origin at least, less a tax than a restitution of the arms and equipment with which he had been provided by his lord during his life and which presumably would be passed on to his successor. The word 'heriot' itself derives from the term *here-geat* or war gear. The rules of this are set out in, for example, Cnut's second code of laws, and are well illustrated in the will of a fairly modest thegn named Ketel (one of the people who made their wills before undertaking a pilgrimage to Rome) in the years shortly before the conquest:

> And I grant to Archbishop Stigand, my lord. . .as my
> heriot a helmet and a coat of mail, and a horse with
> harness, with a sword and a spear.[lvi]

This is clearly the average equipment that the shire levies would be expected to turn up with; a nobleman would have been expected to produce more: at least four horses, more armour and a cash payment as well. We cannot now confirm whether or not Stigand had provided Ketel's equipment in the first place but it is perfectly possible that he did, and it is certain that in most cases it was the lord's responsibility to ensure that the fighters he was responsible for were properly turned out. It is noticeable that, although the Bayeux Tapestry shows what may be unarmed peasants hurling missiles at the battle, there is no indication that most of the regular English troops were less well equipped than their opponents. If it were not for the lavish English moustaches shown by the embroiderers, and for the battle-axes that Normans did not use, it would frequently be difficult to distinguish one side from the other.

All the evidence suggests that the military duty that the shire levies had to provide included service at sea as well as on land, and there are many indications that the men who were summoned to the king's standard were able to fight afloat and that their commanders were as experienced at sea as on land. During the wars against Gruffydd ap Llewellyn in 1062, Harold sailed with the English fleet into Cardigan Bay to attack from the sea while his brother Tostig invaded from Northumbria with land forces, and this was a tactic that had also been used by Athelstan in his campaigns against the Scots. In fact the English did not fight on sea often, and in 1062 Harold may have sailed into Cardigan Bay but then disembarked his men to fight on land. The occasions on which King Alfred tackled the Danes on the water were not his most glorious successes. Nevertheless, Harold was more experienced than Duke William in naval matters, and William of Poitiers emphasizes the fear of the Normans at the prospect of encountering Harold by sea:

> They said. . .he had numerous ships in his fleet and men skilled in nautical arts and hardened in many dangers and sea-battles; and both in wealth and numbers of soldiers his kingdom was greatly superior to their own land. Who could hope that within the prescribed space of one year a fleet could be built, or that oarsmen could be found to man it when it was built?[lvii]

There were complicated regulations governing the provision of ships, but it was clearly a duty that, in an island nation, was laid on all landowners, secular or religious, though many of the great bishoprics and abbeys, especially the inland ones, appear to have commuted their obligations for cash payments with which the king could have ships built on the coast. The last recorded instance of a major ship-building exercise before the conquest is found in the Anglo-Saxon Chronicle (E) in 1009, when Æthelred gave orders for ships to be built all over England, one ship to every 300 hides of land, resulting in a fleet 'greater than any that had ever been seen before in England in any king's day'. He was clearly expecting a new invasion since he ordered them to be built quickly, but, according to the Chronicle, he got little benefit from the expenditure. He and his successors had also relied on mercenary ships, although Edward the Confessor paid off most of these to save money in 1051 and 1052.

Despite the supposedly highly organized feudal nature of pre-conquest Normandy, we know much less about how its armed forces were assembled. It is clear that William had no navy; all Norman accounts emphasize that his first action after taking his decision to invade was to order ships to be built, and it is fairly clear that he also hired and commandeered some. The so-called ship list, which gives details of the numbers of vessels to be contributed by his various nobles, indicates that he must have started pretty well from scratch, and we have to assume that the fleet eventually assembled was varied, some large ships, some small, some transports for stores and equipment, others presumably designed for carrying horses. According to the ship list, about a thousand ships were to be contributed by his nobles, apart from any he may have hired or commandeered, though many of the latter may have been transports; the probable total certainly casts some doubt on the figure of 696 that Wace gives in his *Roman de Rou*, which he tells us he got from his father who was an eyewitness, though Wace is probably nearer the truth than William of Jumièges's 3,000. It may seem strange that a people so recently descended from sea-pirates should apparently have so completely lost touch with the sea, but by the mid-eleventh century Normandy was to all intents and purposes a French province, happy to accommodate the Viking raiders who visited her harbours with booty gained in England and elsewhere but preoccupied with threats from further inland. In this respect, Harold, as William's nervous followers pointed out, had a decided advantage in the possession of a fleet manned by an amphibious force that was certainly more experienced than the Normans were in naval warfare.

Much has been written about the army William raised and its training but in fact little is known of the actual contractual arrangements that produced it. It has been too often supposed that to say that the Norman army was feudal and relied heavily on highly trained cavalry (the existence of the latter being regarded as proof of the former) was sufficient to account for their victory and their imposition of the feudal system on England after the conquest. In essence the feudal system meant that a man paid dues, which could be in services or in grain or some other kind of produce or goods, in return for the land with which he was enfeoffed by his lord, and in this sense the Anglo-Saxon system, as we have seen, was as feudal as the Norman. There would have been in Normandy, as in France generally at the time, the custom of *arrière-ban* by which a ruler could summon his vassals and their own feudatories to battle, but it is uncertain precisely what this meant in pre-conquest Normandy and what it would have produced. There certainly seems to have been some doubt whether it would have obliged vassals to fight overseas. In eleventh-century Normandy, and doubtless in other French provinces, there was a contract between a ruler and his tenants-in-chief by which they would undertake to supply him with a certain number of fighting men when required to do so, but the evidence, pre-1066, for the types of service a tenant was supposed to provide for the 'feudom' he held is extremely sparse, and surviving charters give a very varied and (in military terms) unsatisfactory view of the kind of service likely to be required. There is a dangerous tendency to extrapolate from the more formalized and better recorded systems after the conquest (which, in England at least, were much influenced by pre-conquest English customs) to arrangements in Normandy before 1066, which appear to have been vague and indefinite. In practical terms, as far as the battle of Hastings is concerned, the difference between the so-called Norman feudal system and the English five-hide system seems to have been minimal, and it may be fair to say that the average English and Norman men-at-arms at Hastings would probably not have detected much difference in their conditions of service, except that the Englishman might have been better paid. The difference is that, whereas it is possible to make a theoretical calculation from the hidal system of the maximum number of men an English king could have raised in an emergency, no such calculation is possible in Normandy. The development of the feudal system in England after the conquest owed as much to the pre-conquest English system as to the Norman, William and his immediate successors having found a lot in the English tradition that they did not wish to dispense with – as is indicated by the money-raising machinations of William Rufus already referred to.

The biggest difference between the two armies was the heavy Norman use of cavalry. Much has been made of the absence of English cavalry at Hastings, and of this as further proof of an outdated and obsolescent form of warfare. There was certainly no tradition of cavalry charges in the Anglo-Saxon army, though it is clear from the Chronicle that horses were used to get to the battlefield and to pursue the enemy off it, as at Stamford Bridge. It should be noted that Snorre Sturlason's account of Stamford Bridge in *Heimskringla* says quite clearly that the English fought on horseback there. Snorre's account, however, is so late and in many respects so unreliable that no confidence can be built on his report. Harold could hardly have covered the ground between London and Stamford Bridge as fast as he did if he had not had mounted troops (we have seen that Ketel and his colleagues, if Ketel was typical, were equipped with horses), but to what extent he used horses in the battle that followed is another matter and of that we have no firm evidence. Certainly the account of the struggle to take the bridge over the river implies a fight on foot; if the English had been fighting on horseback, they would surely have been able to have ridden down the lone warrior defending it. Byrhtnoth and his followers rode to the battle of Maldon; but when they got there, Byrhtnoth dismounted and commanded his men to drive away the horses and fight on foot, and this seems to have been the routine procedure. J. H. Clapham, in his essay, 'The Horsing of the Danes',[lviii] which gives an interesting summary of what can be gleaned of the extent to which mounted troops were used throughout the Anglo-Saxon period, maintains that the fighting habits that remained so strong in the century before the conquest represent the racial tradition, unaltered to the end. It should be remembered that, for the past century, the enemies the English had usually had to meet in the battlefield were either Welsh (guerrilla foot fighters *par excellence,* often fighting in hilly country where cavalry would operate at a disadvantage) or Danish or Norwegian raiders who also had the tradition of fighting on foot and certainly did not normally bring warhorses with them, as the Normans did. They helped themselves when they got here when they needed to move fast, as J. H. Clapham points out. If the English had not developed the art of fighting on horseback by 1066, it was largely because they had never needed to.

It should be remembered that when Harold went on campaign with William's troops in Normandy he would have fought on horseback, like his peers, and apparently acquitted himself with distinction. It was probably his first experience of cavalry in action, and it may have had considerable influence on his tactics at Hastings two years later. Even if, after his return to England, he had wanted to create a corps of cavalry to rival the Norman knights, it would have been difficult, if not impossible, for him to do so in time for the invasion. The Norman knights rode stallions (the Bayeux Tapestry makes this unambiguously clear), specially bred over many years and specially trained for fighting; it is unlikely that many comparably suitable horses existed in England at that date, quite apart from the problems there would have been in training their riders in the time available. None the less, Harold's first-hand knowledge of the cavalry tactics he knew he would have to face at Hastings may account in part at least for the defensive position he adopted there. Whatever contempt the Norman cavalry may initially have felt for the English infantry at Hastings, it did not last. In many of the most important battles that the Norman kings were to fight after 1066, they fought on foot – as Henry I did at Tinchebrai, as Stephen did at the battle of Lincoln (though with cavalry on the wings). The lesson of the English shield wall had been learned.

There were differences of approach between England and Normandy. All societies in Europe at this time were military to some extent (it was an aggressive and belligerent period) but not all were obsessed with fighting to the degree that the Normans were. It has been said that 'If not all Norman knights in 1066 were men of substance, it is already true that all great men were knights'.[lix] The corollary is also true: all great men may have been knights, but all knights were certainly not great men nor men of substance. If 'substance' is to be defined here as 'property', most of those who enlisted in William's army, particularly those who were not Norman, certainly weren't. It was property they were signing up for. Many 'knights' were little more than mounted thugs. Precisely how to define the word 'knight' in 1066 is controversial – it was certainly not as formalized as it would be by the time of Malory or even Chaucer – but it did indicate a man who fought on horseback and had undergone a long and arduous training to do so. Whether he did so as a condition of the land he held or was a sword for hire was immaterial. Indeed, the very derivation of the word 'knight' is suggestive. There seems to have been no precise Norman-French equivalent for it other than the purely descriptive word 'chevalier', one who goes on horseback – who need not, of course, be a military man at all. In the Latin chronicles, which are what we have principally to rely on, a knight would frequently simply have been referred to as *miles*, a word with a wide range of possible applications (William of Poitiers uses *miles* and *equites* indifferently). The word 'knight', so redolent of chivalry and romance today, derives from the Old English *cniht*, a serving man or serving boy, possibly because that was how they were seen, post-conquest, by the English in their relationship to the lord who employed them.

Yet, for a people so obsessed by war, the overall picture regarding obligations for military service in Normandy before the conquest does seem to be obscure and messy, by comparison with England. The situation has been summarized by Marjorie Chibnall who, after describing the general arrangements as far as they can be deduced, points out that

> there is no clear proof of any general system of military quotas imposed from above; or of an accepted norm for feudal services and obligations, legally enforceable on the initiative of either side in a superior ducal court – and this surely is a necessary corollary for any accepted general norm. It is at least arguable that the services owed were either relics of older, Carolingian obligations, or the outcome of individual life contracts between different lords and their vassals, and that their systematization was the result only of the intense military activity of the period of the conquest, and the very slow development of a common law in the century after it.[lx]

In other words, the feudal customs to which William's victory has often been ascribed were the result, not the cause, of the conquest. This makes the calculation of what William might have been able to call on within his own duchy very difficult; that it was insufficient for the enterprise we know, since he advertised widely for mercenaries throughout Europe. It is hardly surprising if one compares the size of Normandy with the size of England: William, the vassal of the King of France, controlled an area only a little larger than the earldom of East Anglia held by Harold, the vassal of the King of England, before the death of his father and smaller than the earldom of Wessex he held after it, let alone the totality of the kingdom of England. In theory, since the size of territory had a direct effect on the number of men who could be expected from it, Harold should have been able to raise an army many times the size of anything William could bring against it from Normandy. In fact, the situation at Hastings was complicated by many other factors, as we shall see. One document does give a rough indication of the components of William's army: this is the penitential code drawn up in 1070 by Bishop Ermenfrid, according to which the sins of those who fought in the Norman army were to be expiated. It distinguishes between those who William had armed, those who had armed themselves, those who owed him military service for the lands they held and those who fought for pay. There is no way now of establishing how many men fell into the various categories; the Bretons seem to have formed a large contingent, presumably fighting for pay, and it is notable that they continued to fight as mercenaries for William in his later career and for his sons.

We know most about the training and equipment of those who fought on horseback. It was the custom, in Normandy as in other parts of France, for a boy of good family to be sent for a knightly education in the household of the ruler (if the boy was of sufficiently elevated rank) or of one of the great lords, and he would presumably find himself there in the company of other boys of his own age and rank, all training for the same future. It was rather like going to public school. The lord who undertook the training of the youngsters would have the pick of them to join his household retainers in due course. From their ranks he would provide the knights who would be called for by his own lord when he needed an army; those whom he did not need or want, or who did not wish to remain with him, would probably have found employment elsewhere quite easily. Those of them who were eldest sons would in due course inherit family estates and would then look for their own retainers. The younger sons on the whole had to fend for themselves, and large numbers of them did so outside Normandy – in Spain, in Byzantium, and most of all in Italy. The Norman conquest of Apulia was largely the work of younger sons of noble families, looking for lands and heiresses outside their homeland. While they were training they would learn horsemanship, the use of weapons, the techniques of war and, in theory at least, manners and chivalric behaviour. They would be trained in hunting and tournament, the main education and diversion of the knightly families if there did not happen to be a war in progress. And they would learn to fight together as a team, usually in squadrons, or *conrois,* of ten.

The costs of a knightly profession were high. A young man would not, unless he were extremely lucky, be considered for employment by any lord unless he possessed a hauberk or coat of mail, helmet, shield, sword, lance and at least one well-trained war-horse, preferably more (in fact, very similar equipment to that of the English thegn Ketel). But this would be the minimum. Moreover, he would need an esquire or servant of some kind who would also have to be mounted, and presumably a baggage horse as well. All these things were extremely expensive and, in time of war, would frequently have to be replaced. William is said to have had three horses killed under him at Hastings, and this cannot have been unusual. To some extent, replacements could be found on the battlefield. The discrepancies between the differently shaped shields (some round, some kite-shaped) of the English at Hastings, as illustrated in the Bayeux Tapestry, have been hypothetically attributed to the fact that the bearers of the round shields had replaced their damaged kite-shaped shields with those of the dead Norwegians at Stamford Bridge, since round shields were used in Scandinavia later than in England; the borders of the Tapestry show Norman soldiers stripping the English dead of hauberks and swords in the later stages of the battle. But if a father wanted to send his younger son out into the world as a freelance knight, he would have had to spend a great deal of money on his initial equipment. It was to the freelances of this kind that William looked to make up his ranks, and it is not hard to see how his promises of land and wealth in England attracted them.

What the system did produce was an excessive number of testosterone-fuelled young men, unqualified and unsuited for any profession other than fighting and killing, and regarding any other occupation as below their dignity. While the average English thegn, when not required for the defence of his country, would perfectly happily settle back into a routine of agriculture and possibly even a little trade, the young Norman knight would have regarded any such occupations as totally inconsistent with his chivalric training. It is this outlook that explains the large number of necessitous Norman knights that are to be found in the wars of southern Italy, Spain, Constantinople, the Crusades later on – and, of course, in William's army.

We know least about the infantry parts of his army. We know that he did have foot soldiers, with and without body armour, and also quantities of archers; it has been estimated that he probably had no more than 2,500 cavalry. The infantry would have formed the largest part of his force. It is less clear where they came from and on what basis they were raised. Some of them were probably mercenaries, like the freelance knights, but what kind of training and experience they had (especially the archers) and how they were found is not so easy to establish. If some of them came as part of the service provided by his barons and landowners, what were the terms on which they were sent? Who was responsible for their keep? There seems to have been no such clear arrangement for their provision and payment as there was in the English hidal system. William of Poitiers makes it clear that in this particular case the duke himself paid for their keep to prevent them from ravaging his land for subsistence (he does not say whether they were paid anything more than that, and one must deduce that his promises of money and land in England were in lieu of more orthodox payment), but this cannot always have been so; indeed, it is implied that it was an exceptional arrangement. In enemy territory, of course, they would be expected to live off the land, as they did after they landed in Sussex. But if they were on campaign within Normandy, during the invasions of the King of France, for example, how were they normally maintained? Off the land again, one must suppose. They may, in everyday life, have been professional men-at-arms, huntsmen, peasants; we can only guess. There is nothing to show where the infantry came from or under what conditions they served, and yet they formed the greater part of the army. One of the most remarkable of William's achievements during the invasion was that he managed to keep his men together during the lengthy period at Dives and St Valéry while he was waiting for favourable winds without allowing any plundering or foraging. To organize a commissariat on this scale must have been a mammoth job, and awed calculations have been made of the amount of meat, grain and ale that would have been necessary for the men, of the amount of fodder for the horses, and of the tons of excrement, human and equine, that would have had to be disposed of in the interests of health (B. S. Bachrach estimated 9,000 cartloads of grain, straw, wine and firewood, 700,000 gallons of urine from the horses and 5 million pounds of horse-droppings, for a month's stay[lxi]). Yet, if we are to believe William of Poitiers, he did it, and 'the cattle and flocks of the people of the province grazed safely, whether in the fields or on the waste. The crops waited unharmed for the scythe of the harvester, and were neither trampled by the proud stampede of horsemen nor cut down by foragers'.[lxii] It was indeed a remarkable achievement, and one in which William is considered to have outgeneralled his rival, who had to disband his forces in August through lack of food. Still, Harold had held his together for four months, a longer period.

In the end, the outcome was determined not by what each man might normally have been able to raise, but by circumstances. If Harold fought at Hastings without archers (one small miserable archer is shown in the English ranks in the Bayeux Tapestry, almost in mockery, though it has been suggested that his appearance is symbolic in character, and that he represented a larger contingent), it was almost certainly because he had used them at Stamford Bridge (the Norwegian king was killed by an arrow), and could not get them south quickly enough, or could not get fresh men in time. Whether they would have made a difference to the final result can never be known.

BATTLE OF HASTINGS | 116

It may be helpful to add a brief note on the armour and equipment that both sides would have had.[lxiii] The term 'body armour' may imply more to twenty-first century ears than it meant to eleventh-century wearers. For many soldiers, a coat of mail or hauberk probably merely signified metal rings sewn to a leather or boiled leather foundation. For those of higher rank, the hauberk was more likely to be interlinked chain-mail, worn over some sort of padded undergarment, which both cushioned blows and protected the body from having the mail driven into it by sword or axe cuts. Sometimes the hauberk incorporated a sort of hood, which protected the neck and was covered by the helmet. This is, interestingly, one way in which the Bayeux Tapestry designer seems to betray his English nationality. He depicts both sides in hauberks that appear to be trousered. These would have been very impractical (indeed, agonizing) for cavalry wear; the Norman hauberks would probably have been skirted, slashed fore and rear, so that they would divide on horseback and protect the legs. This is borne out by the story that when William was arming on the morning of the battle, he was accidentally handed his hauberk back to front and put it on over his head that way. The English, on the other hand, fighting on foot, did indeed need the trousered variety to protect the groin and other areas that would be more vulnerable. How the wearer got into and out of this kind of mail is still a matter of conjecture. The problem is not solved by the pictures of the Norman soldiers stripping the English dead in the final scenes of the Tapestry. Snorre Sturlason tells us that Harald Hardrada's coat of mail 'was called Emma. It was so long that it reached below his knee, and so strong that no weapon could pierce it'.[lxiv] He was probably not wearing it at Stamford Bridge, but Emma would not have saved him in any event; he was reportedly killed by an arrow in the throat.

Helmets were conical and made of iron, with a nose-piece at the front (clearly shown in the Tapestry) and, in some cases, a metal flap or curtain of mail at the back or sides to protect the neck and cheeks; they seem to have been identical for all ranks. Surviving examples are either cast in one piece, with the addition of the nose-piece and neck-protector, or are constructed from four joined plates coming together in a point at the top and bound by metal or possibly, in some cases, leather, around the head at the foot. Some of those found have traces inside that suggest that they were sometimes lined or padded. Such a helmet is a far cry from the magnificence of the reconstructed Sutton Hoo helmet; but this was more likely to have been a piece of royal regalia (primitive kings are thought to have been crowned with a helmet rather than the later crown, a symbol of their role as protector of their people) than a working helmet. It probably never saw service on the battlefield.

The shield would have been made of wood (lime was generally favoured), covered in many cases with leather and edged with either leather or metal. A round hole in the centre was fitted with a metal boss (round or conical) that covered the grip for the hand and could be used for thrusting. Towards the end of *Beowulf,* the aged hero orders a shield of iron to be made for his last fight with the dragon, knowing that a wooden shield would provide little protection from the beast's fiery breath. That the English army at Hastings still had wooden shields is indicated by the Tapestry's portrayal of the Norman arrows piercing them like pincushions; arrows would have been more likely to have rebounded from metal shields. William of Poitiers' remark that the English battle-axes had no difficulty in shearing through them suggests that the Normans also used wooden ones.

As for weapons, it is clear from the Tapestry that the Norman knights charged with spears or javelins rather than the lances that became the chief cavalry weapon very shortly afterwards. The ones we see are sometimes wielded overarm, for throwing or piercing, sometimes underarm, as the lance would later be held. But the weight of the couched lance and the discipline of the concerted charge that could pierce the walls of Babylon, as Anna Comnena, the historian daughter of Byzantine Emperor Alexius I, was later to write, were not available at Hastings. There was probably little difference between the spears carried by the two sides. Some surviving spears have wings a short way below the head, presumably to prevent the weapon penetrating so deeply that it could not be drawn out and reused. It was obviously a weapon common to all ranks; it was part of the basic equipment of the English thegn Ketel, and Duke William was found with a broken spear in his hand at the end of the battle. Snorre Sturlason gives an account of Harald Hardrada's instructions to his men at Stamford Bridge: 'those in the front rank are to set their spear-shafts into the ground and turn the points towards the riders' breasts when they charge us; and those immediately behind are to set their spears against the horses' chests.'[lxv] Since it is almost certain that the English did not fight on horseback at Stamford Bridge, this has been read as a confused memory of what actually happened at Hastings; at any rate, it is a very plausible account of how spears were used by the English there.

The most feared English weapon was the two-handed bearded axe (so called because of the shape of the blade), the weapon of choice of the housecarls but of other warriors as well, since the king is shown with one in his hand as he is cut down. Indeed, he is shown carrying one earlier, when he is offered the crown, which suggests that some royal or sacramental association may have attached to the axe. In battle, it was normally wielded to strike from the left, to attack the side of the opponent that was not protected by his shield, but in fact it must easily have cut through wood and even through chain-mail, as reported by William of Poitiers. The biggest disadvantage of the axe was that, since it had to be swung with both hands, the axeman could not use his shield to protect himself (unless it was simply hung around his neck), and was therefore very vulnerable at the top of his swing. It is possible that the line included spearmen interspersed among the axemen, who, fighting in the way Snorre described, could provide some cover for them. In addition to this fearsome weapon, there would have been smaller lighter axes for hand-to-hand fighting and for throwing. One weapon that seems to have been peculiar to the Normans at the battle was the mace. The Tapestry shows both William and his half-brother, Odo, Bishop of Bayeux, carrying what appear to be club-like maces, but these may have been symbols of authority (perhaps ancestors of the field-marshal's baton) rather than weapons.

As for swords, all free men who could afford them would have carried them, Norman and English, and there were enormous variations in quality and strength. It was very much a question of what you had inherited or what you could pay. Those of the English who did not aspire to a double-edged sword, and no doubt also many of those who did, probably carried the *seax*, a sort of single-edged cutlass or long dagger.

One last point needs to be noted. Snorre Sturlason, in his account of the battle of Stamford Bridge, speaks of the English horses of the housecarls wearing chain-mail. There is no hint in the Bayeux Tapestry of any kind of protection, chain-mail or otherwise, for the Norman horses. If armour for horses was generally in use in 1066, and the English mounts had it, it is incomprehensible that the cavalry-obsessed Normans should not have had it too. By the time Snorre wrote two centuries later, its availability would have been taken for granted. His assumption that it was available in 1066 is a further reminder that we should not be seduced by his readability.

THE PROLOGUE

The length of time Harold spent in Normandy is as unknown as its precise date or, indeed, its purpose. All that is known is that he was back in England in 1065. 'Before Lammas' (1 August), according to the Anglo-Saxon Chronicle, he ordered the building of a hunting lodge at Portskewet in Wales, so that the king (who was presumably at that time in good health) could hunt there; but on 24 August the site was overrun by Caradoc ap Gruffydd and the workmen killed. In September, more serious trouble broke out. In Northumbria, where Harold's brother, Tostig, had been earl since 1055, there had been unrest on account of his harsh rule. Whether Tostig was really harsh or simply enforcing laws that had fallen into disuse under his predecessor, Earl Siward, cannot now be known; he is described by the author of the *Vita Ædwardi* as 'a little over-zealous in attacking evil', which perhaps implies a combination of the two. The Northumbrians seem to have had a good case: according to Florence of Worcester, the immediate cause of the rising was Tostig's slaying of two Northumbrian nobles who were in his house under safe conduct, and the murder at court of Gospatric, a member of the old Northumbrian ruling house, in which he rather discreditably implicated his sister, Queen Edith, who organized it for him. Certainly, he seems to have doubled the taxes, which alone would be enough to cause unrest. On 3 October, while he was at court with the king, the Northumbrians rose up and killed as many of his housecarls and servants as they could find, broke open his treasury and carried off all his effects. They repudiated Tostig and sent a summons to Morcar, brother of Edwin, Earl of Mercia since the exile and death of their father Ælfgar, to be their earl; led by him, the Northumbrians advanced into England where they were joined by Edwin with his Mercian troops and some Welsh reinforcements. At Northampton they were met by Harold, sent by the king to try to effect some kind of reconciliation, but on this occasion his diplomatic powers failed. The Northumbrians refused point blank to take Tostig back. Edward tried to call out the army, as he had done in 1051, to restore Tostig by force of arms but found that on this occasion they would not fight. Confronted by the armed forces of all Northumbria and Mercia, and with a general feeling elsewhere in the country that Tostig had come by his deserts, the king had little alternative but to give in. The meeting was adjourned to Oxford where, after the feast of All Saints (1 November), Edward was obliged to agree to the exiling of Tostig and his replacement as earl by Morcar, and swore to uphold the laws of Cnut.

These events raise some interesting points, in addition to the fact that the outlawing of Tostig was almost certainly indirectly responsible for the defeat at Hastings. Firstly, although much is made of the separateness and of the Scandinavian sympathies of the inhabitants of the Danelaw, of which Northumbria was the most important part, there seems to have been no idea of any claim for independence in the rising. The Northumbrians did not want to leave the kingdom of England, they simply wanted a different earl – and the earl whom they chose, in preference to the half-Danish Tostig, was a man with no Danish blood in his veins at all. Even Cnut, a Danish king, had had difficulty with his relations with Northumbria; it was a turbulent region. Secondly, it has been suggested that the demand for the reaffirmation of the laws of Cnut indicates a demand for specifically Danish legislation for Northumbria alone; it is more likely that, since Edward, unlike so many of his predecessors, had never issued a law-code, and Harold Harefoot and Harthacnut had never had time to do so, the laws of Cnut were presumably the legal code in force over all England throughout his reign. The laws of King Edward, that the Conqueror was later symbolically to invoke, were in fact the laws of an earlier conqueror. The laws of Cnut were actually written for him by the impeccably English Archbishop Wulfstan of York and were based on the earlier laws of King Edgar. Patrick Wormald has surmised that the significance of Cnut's law for the Northumbrian rebels was that it represented the pattern of northern rule subverted by Tostig's government, and that their invocation of Cnut, like the Conqueror's of Edward, was as much symbolic as practical; this seems likely.[lxvi] Thirdly, the insurrection caused an insuperable breach between Harold and Tostig, who blamed his brother for not supporting him and (if the *Vita Ædwardi* is to be believed) accused him in public of fomenting the rising to injure him. Finally, it is clear from Harold's activities at Portskewet that the king was at that time in good enough health to be able to contemplate a hunting break there.

This was soon to change. According to the *Vita Ædwardi,* both Edward and the queen became ill with grief over the loss of Tostig, and a more modern biographer has guessed that the king may have suffered one or more strokes as a result of the stress.[lxvii] From this point on, his health declined steadily. Tostig, meanwhile, sought refuge once again in Flanders, and cast around for allies to support his restoration. He is said (there is no firm evidence) to have tried Normandy, but if he did, he got no direct help from William, who may none the less have been pleased enough to encourage him to add to Harold's problems. He tried Denmark, but his cousin, Sweyn Estrithson, pleaded other commitments. He did rather better in Norway with Harald Hardrada.

In the meantime, the king's health continued to decline. His condition worsened on Christmas Eve, but he was able to hold his normal Christmas court, though in London, rather than the usual Gloucester, partly because of his health, but also because his new foundation at Westminster was to be consecrated during the festival. But when it came to the day of consecration, he was too ill to attend and the ceremony was performed in his absence. The double ceremony, Christmas and the consecration, combined with the king's failing health, no doubt accounts for the large assembly there was in London over the festival. Charter lists issued over the period make it clear that virtually everyone of consequence in the country was there – English, Scandinavian, French, Norman, lay and cleric. As Frank Barlow has pointed out, it was not an assembly that could have been intimidated or overawed: 'It was thoroughly representative of the various interests in the land, and any decision it took can be considered the voice of the kingdom'.[lxviii] On 5 January, according to the *Vita Ædwardi,* after having recounted to those standing about him a dream that prophesied disaster to the kingdom on account of the sins of the people and the Church, the king spoke his last will and testament, commending his widow and servants, with the kingdom, to Harold's care. It has been argued by many, then and now, that his words could be construed as asking Harold to care for them as proxy for the true heir; if that is so, it is extremely strange that he should not have named that heir since his nomination would have been required before his nominee could have been ratified by the

Witan, the final and crucial step. But we must sympathize with the predicament in which the anonymous author of the *Vita Ædwardi* found himself at this point. Precisely when he wrote is not known but certainly by the time he reached this stage in his narrative, Hastings had been fought and the Normans had won. It is to this hindsight that the relevance of the king's strange dream has been attributed. William was established on the throne and Harold was declared a usurper. Certainly a little ambiguity of wording in the recording of the king's last speech is understandable in the circumstances; and we must allow for the fact that the king's last words were probably retailed to the author by the queen, the commissioner of her husband's biography, and the person to whom the author would most naturally look for information on this important point. Her views on her brother's succession are believed to be equally ambiguous. Florence of Worcester reports the fact without any uncertainty:

> On Thursday the vigil of our Lord's Epiphany. . .the pacific king, Edward, son of King Ethelred, died at London, having reigned over the English twenty-three years six months and seven days. The next day he was buried in kingly style amid the bitter lamentations of all present. After his burial the under-king, Harold, son of Earl Godwine, whom the king had nominated as his successor, was chosen king by the chief magnates of all England; and on the same day Harold was crowned with great ceremony by Aldred, archbishop of York.[lxix]

What is notable is that no other candidate than Harold seems to have been put forward at this stage. The king's last word was important, but not overridingly so. If he had bequeathed his kingdom to an unacceptable candidate, perhaps more significance would have been attached to Stigand's whisper at the deathbed (as the king recounted his dream) that the old man was raving. As it is, no party seems to have supported the claims of the boy Atheling; no other candidate is even mentioned. Harold appears to have been elected unopposed by the Witan; it would be the last occasion until 1689 on which an English king owed his title not to hereditary descent but to the will of the people as represented by the chief men assembled in council. He was, as Ann Williams concludes after assessing the evidence, a popular choice for the kingship.[lxx] He was crowned by Ealdred, Archbishop of York, the day after (some say the same day as) Edward's burial in his new church, Westminster Abbey, probably in the same building. According to William of Poitiers, Stigand performed the ceremony; but according to William of Poitiers, Harold was elected by 'a few ill-disposed partisans'. Harold would have been very careful to avoid coronation by Stigand for the same reason as he seems to have avoided asking him to consecrate his new church at Waltham: Stigand was under papal interdict, and his actions as archbishop could therefore have been seen as invalid. Although written down later, the testimony of Florence of Worcester, who would have obtained his information from those who were present at the ceremony (probably his own bishop, Wulfstan, since Ealdred himself, previously Bishop of Worcester, had died in 1069), is far more satisfactory.

The coronation ceremony followed hard on the heels of Edward's funeral for reasons of practical convenience. Coronations normally took place at the great feasts of the Church. That Christmas, all the magnates who should be present on such an occasion were gathered in London and would disperse after the funeral. They could probably not be reassembled until Easter. Kings in the past had waited longer than from Epiphany to Easter to be hallowed, but on this occasion, with the various threats facing the kingdom, it was desirable that there should be a king on the throne, properly consecrated and acclaimed, who could speak with authority for the people. At no stage does it seem to have been disputed, even by William of Poitiers, that Edward had indeed named Harold as his successor, and it would not have been difficult for a different story to be circulated after the conquest if any of those who had been present and survived had cared to do so. And in fact all those whom we know to have been at the deathbed (with the exception of Harold himself) did survive the conquest: the queen, Stigand and Robert FitzWymark (a cousin of both Edward and William) were all alive and able to give evidence if they had wished to. None seems to have done so, not even FitzWymark who clearly favoured the Norman takeover, or the queen who is reputed to have done so.

A point of interest about Edward's death and Harold's election is the fact that William was not there. He had ample opportunities for getting news from England, and it would be most surprising if he had not heard by Christmas that the king was failing fast. There were no such reasons in 1065 as there had been in 1051 to keep him in Normandy. If he truly believed that he was Edward's chosen heir, nothing could have been more natural than that he should go immediately to attend his cousin's last moments and receive his final deathbed nomination. It would have been his best chance of a peaceful succession. It can be argued that he placed his trust in Harold's oath to represent his interests and support his election. But it seems strangely unlike William to trust a rival to that extent.

At the opening of Harold's reign, life seems to have continued normally. Again, the situation is described by Florence of Worcester in fulsome terms:

On taking the helm of the kingdom Harold immediately began to abolish unjust laws and to make good ones; to patronise churches and monasteries; to pay particular reverence to bishops, abbots, monks and clerks; and to show himself pious, humble and affable to all good men. But he treated malefactors with great severity, and gave general orders to his earls, ealdormen, sheriffs and thegns to imprison all thieves, robbers and disturbers of the kingdom. He laboured in his own person by sea and by land for the protection of his realm.[lxxi]

Few records of Harold's short reign survive, for obvious reasons; no one, after Hastings, would want to produce any of his charters or writs in evidence, and in fact only one writ has survived. But from what indications there are, there is no reason to doubt the general tenor of Florence of Worcester's remarks. Of the few tangible pieces of evidence that survive, the most impressive is his coinage, elegant silver pennies of good weight, bearing his crowned head in profile, struck in more than forty mints. The number of coins minted indicates the urgent need he felt he was likely to have for ready money.

Trouble began in the late spring. On 24 April Halley's comet made its appearance, causing wonder and consternation on both sides of the Channel. Shortly after, the exiled Tostig appeared with a fleet, pillaged along the south coast from Wight to Sandwich, pressganging men as he went, and, scared off by King Harold's arrival, continued up to Lindsey where he is said to have burnt many villages and put many men to death. There he was encountered by Earls Edwin and Morcar, who beat him off with much loss. Most of his remaining men deserted, and he limped with his remaining twelve small ships up to Scotland where he was sheltered by King Malcolm, his sworn brother.

In the meantime, the main activity shifted to Normandy. William must have got early news of Harold's coronation. William of Poitiers tells how he consulted the Norman barons who at first discouraged an armed attack on England, thinking it beyond the resources of Normandy, but were brought by their confidence in his judgement to agree; how he set in hand the building of ships; how he received the many foreign knights who came to join his standard, 'attracted partly by the well-known liberality of the duke, but all fully confident of the justice of his cause'.[lxxii]

His diplomatic efforts, however, were no less intensive than his military preparations. According to his biographer,

> The chronology of the duke's acts during the earlier half
> of 1066 is somewhat confused, but their nature and
> purpose is clear, as is also the ultimate end to which they
> were all so steadfastly directed. During this critical
> interval, Duke William of Normandy secured the
> support of his vassals. He fostered divisions among his
> rivals. He successfully appealed to the public opinion of
> Europe. And he made the preparations essential for
> equipping the expedition which was, at last, to take him
> to victory overseas.[lxxiii]

He was in a particularly favourable position in 1066. If Edward had died ten years earlier, it is possible that William would have felt it too risky to invade England. In 1056 he had just repelled the latest in a series of joint attacks by his overlord the King of France and the Count of Anjou; in 1060 both died. The former left a boy as his heir, and appointed as his regent and guardian the Count of Flanders who was William's father-in-law; the latter had no direct heir and left Anjou to be contested between two nephews. By 1066 William had secured possession of Maine and the Vexin, which safeguarded his southern borders; he was overlord of Ponthieu on his eastern flank, Flanders under his father-in-law was unlikely to be any threat to him and even the erratic Count of Brittany to his west, who took the opportunity of William's venture to stake a claim to Normandy, died conveniently (reputedly by poison) while preparations for the invasion were in progress. Neither the Breton count's death nor William's recent campaign there appears to have harmed his reputation among the Bretons, judging by the number of them who fought at Hastings. He controlled all the Channel ports from the river Coesnon to the Flemish frontier. Within Normandy, he had formed a tight network of landed magnates, all allied to him by kin or by interest, to the oldest of whom he could confide the oversight of his duchess (nominally his regent), his heir and his duchy during his absence. None of his predecessors had ever felt himself as secure in Normandy as William did in the summer of 1066. It is a proof of his efficacy that he was able to undertake the English invasion without any attempt, internal or external, being made on his power at home. But luck favoured him too. He could not have dictated the deaths of the French king and Martel; nor could he have foreseen the chance that had delivered Harold into his hands, nor the rising that led to Tostig's outlawing and caused a weak spot at the heart of England at the worst possible moment. Indeed, if Edward had died in 1063, not 1066, William's situation would have been much weaker; at that stage, Harold had not made his ill-fated journey, had sworn no oaths and the bond between the two Godwinson brothers had not been broken. But Edward did not die in 1063; he died in 1066, at the moment most favourable to William's ambition.

Duke William did not delay in appealing to public opinion in

Bayeux Tapestry (plate 1): Earl Harold talks with King Edward before setting out on his journey to Normandy. Note that there is no indication of the subject of their conversation.

Bayeux Tapestry (plate 26): 'Where Harold makes his oath to Duke William'.

Jumièges Abbey Church, on which it is thought that Edward the Confessor's Westminster Abbey was modelled.

Bayeux Tapestry (plate 28): '[Harold] comes to Edward'. Harold's conversation with the king when he returns from Normandy.

Hinged clasp from the Sutton Hoo burial mound; these objects are characteristic of the exquisite jewellery made by the Anglo-Saxons: the cloisonné work, set with garnets, is thought to have been typical of Kent. The clasp, when closed, is curved, probably to fit the shoulder.

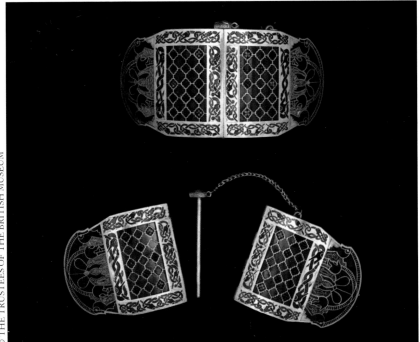

Bayeux Tapestry (plate 31): 'Here sits Harold, King of the English'. The coronation of Harold. Archbishop Stigand is shown beside him, with the implication that he crowned him.

Harold's coinage. On the reverse side, the silver penny bears the single word, *Pax*, 'peace'. The king's crowned head, though obviously designed to symbolize majesty, shows more indications of being an attempt at a realistic likeness than most earlier English coins.

Top: Bayeux Tapestry (plate 71): 'Here King Harold is killed'.
Above: Bayeux Tapestry (plate 72): 'And the English turn in flight'.

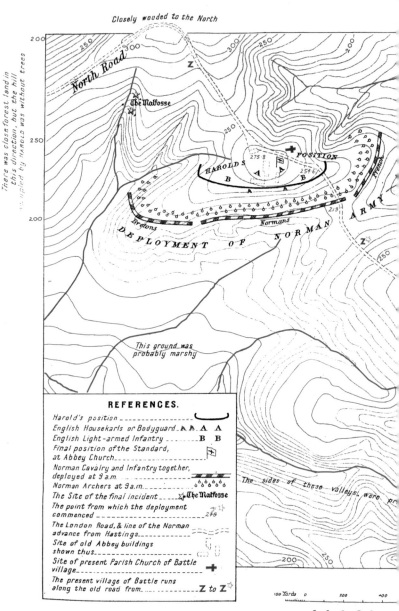

Closely wooded to the North

North Road

There was close forest land in this direction, but the hill on which by HAROLD was without trees

The Malfosse

Z

HAROLD'S POSITION

DEPLOYMENT OF NORMAN ARMY

Bretons

Normans

This ground was probably marshy

The sides of these valleys, were pr

REFERENCES.

Harold's position _____
English Housekarls or Bodyguard ▲ ▲ ▲ ▲
English Light-armed Infantry _____ **B B**
Final position of the Standard, at Abbey Church _____
Norman Cavalry and Infantry together, deployed at 9 a.m. _____
Norman Archers at 9 a.m. _____
The Site of the final incident _____✗ The Malfosse
The point from which the deployment commenced _____
The London Road, & line of the Norman advance from Hastings _____
Site of old Abbey buildings shown thus _____
Site of present Parish Church of Battle village _____ ✚
The present village of Battle runs along the old road from _____ Z to Z

100 Yards 0   200   400

Scale Six Inches to
Contours at 10

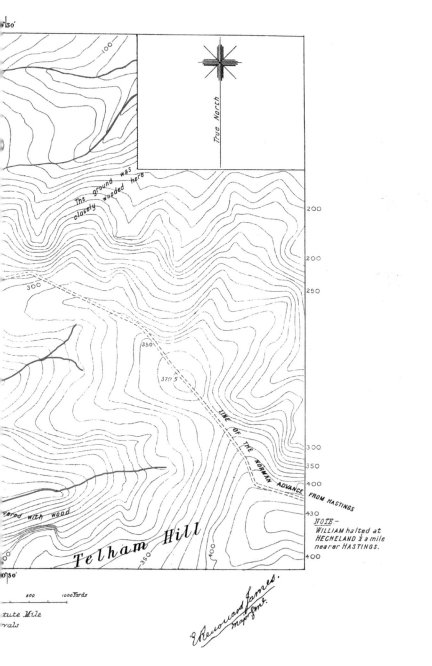

True North

The ground was closely wooded here

200

200

250

300

350

370 5

LINE OF THE NORMAN ADVANCE FROM HASTINGS

300

350

400

430

400

NOTE.—
WILLIAM halted at
HECHELAND ¼ a mile
nearer HASTINGS.

vered with wood

Telham Hill

350

400

'0'50'

600   1000 Yards

tute Mile
vals

E.Reuouard James.
Map Junc.

The Benedictional of St Æthelwold (painted at his command 'with numerous beautiful colours and with gold' at Winchester between 971 and 984): the three kings present their gifts to the infant Christ.

Europe; according to William of Poitiers, he sent delegations to the Holy Roman Emperor and to the King of Denmark; what answer he received from the empire is not known, probably at best neutral, but it appears that Sweyn Estrithson sent men to the support of his cousin Harold rather than to William. But these were comparatively small fish. His most important appeal was to the Pope. His delegate to the Vatican is said to have been Gilbert, Archdeacon of Lisieux. No records of his appeal have survived, but it is not difficult to imagine its grounds: his promise from the late king and Harold's oath and perjury would have formed the central plank of it, but there would have been more. And for an understanding of what he could offer and what the Pope could offer him, we must look at the situation in the Vatican in 1066.

The occupant of the papal chair at that time was Pope Alexander II, who had succeeded Nicholas II in 1061. The short reign of Nicholas had been marked especially by three policies: the energetic pushing forward of the movement for ecclesiastical and monastic reform, the transfer of the responsibility for the election of the Pope to the College of Cardinals; and an intensification of the Vatican's relationship with the Normans of southern Italy. In all of these Nicholas had the vigorous support of Cardinal Hildebrand, himself to succeed Alexander II in 1073 under the name of Gregory VII. Hildebrand's power under his two predecessors was enormous; once he had succeeded, his ambitions went much further than earlier popes would have contemplated. His reign has been described by the historian of Europe, H. A. L. Fisher:

> With imperious courage Hildebrand conceived of the
> world as a single Christian polity governed by an

omnipotent and infallible Pope, a Pope bound by no
laws, by whom an offending prince might be driven
from his throne, cut off from the sacraments of the
church, and severed from the allegiance of his subjects.
Believing that the time had now come to reconstruct the
militia of the Catholic church, he preached the doctrine
of a celibate clergy under the undivided control of the
Vicar of Christ. At one and the same time he was
prepared in the interests of an autonomous clerical
profession to break up the family life of the German
clergy and to sap the power of the German king. His
claims were exorbitant.[lxxiv]

What Fisher does not mention is the third plank of the papal policy
under Nicholas II, the link with the Normans of southern Italy.
The infiltration of the southern states, then a multiracial if
turbulent mix of Greeks, Saracens and the indigenous inhabitants,
had been started about 1000 by bands of younger sons of Norman
families, hungry for land and wealth. They operated at first as
mercenaries, selling their swords to whichever ruler in the war-
torn district paid best. The arrival in the 1030s of several younger
sons of the minor Norman baron Tancred de Hauteville, changed
the situation; from then on, the Normans fought for themselves.
By 1066 the de Hautevilles dominated southern Italy and Sicily,
and their leader, Robert Guiscard, had in 1059 been invested by the
Vatican with the titles of Duke of Apulia and Calabria and King
of Sicily, in return for oaths of fealty and promises of assistance to
the Holy See. The methods by which he attained this eminence are
perhaps best indicated by Dante, who compares a sight in the eighth
circle of hell in which countless shades lie horribly wounded with
a battlefield on which Robert Guiscard had fought. The alliance

between Hildebrand and the Italian Normans in the papal battles against other enemies, which may be compared to the policy of casting out devils through the prince of devils (or indeed to Æthelred's policy of hiring one lot of Vikings to cast out another), was to rebound upon Gregory VII in due course; in 1066 it still held good, to the extent that Norman priorities mattered to the Vatican and could, when necessary, be enforced.

This was not only because Guiscard and his cohorts were in effect the protectors of the papacy. As part of the ecclesiastical reform movement, the campaign against the heathen that very shortly afterwards was to lead to the first Crusade was already gathering strength and enthusiasm. Norman mercenaries who fought the Saracens in Spain did so as soldiers of Christ. In Italy, the Norman campaigns against the Muslims in Sicily were conducted with papal blessing to 'win back to the worship of the true God a land given over to infidelity', according to William of Malmesbury. The first Crusade was not to be preached until 1095, but the spirit that caused thousands of knights all over Europe to enlist in it was already widely disseminated. The prospect, therefore, of a venture that combined the virtue of a religious mission to bring down a perjurer and usurper and to bring spiritual health to the Church in England with the promise of land and booty was irresistible.

The closeness of the assumptions and theories that underpinned the first Crusade to those that supported the conquest is uncanny. As the Pope launched the Crusade, so, we are told, he blessed the conquest. Where those who preached the Crusade declared that infidels were untrustworthy and unfit to rule Christians, so William maintained that Harold was forsworn and, as a usurper, unfit to rule over England. As Crusaders were promised God's aid and absolution for past sins and the wealth of the conquered infidels, so were the soldiers of fortune who enlisted in William's army (indeed, William pointed out to his mercenary recruits that whereas he had the power to promise Harold's lands and wealth to his followers, Harold had no power to give anything of William's to his men). As the main objective of the Crusade was to rescue the holy places of the east and the Christians who worshipped in them, so one of the main objectives of the conquest was to be the reform of the English Church.

There was, in fact, little wrong with the English Church. For centuries, indeed, there had been a particularly close relationship between the English Church and the papacy. Since before the time of Alfred Rome had been regarded as the mother church by Anglo-Saxon England. The origin of the voluntary tax paid to the Pope (known variously as Peter's pence, Rome-Scot, hearth-scot) by England is unknown, but it is thought to have started in the reign of Alfred; no other Christian country paid it. Most of the English payment was appropriated by the reigning Pope, though part is thought to have gone to the Church in the English quarter in Rome, known by the English as their *burh* or borough, a name supposedly perpetuated in the present Roman *Borgo*. Alfred had secured exemption from taxation for this area, and Pope Leo IX had acknowledged its right to bury all Englishmen who came and died there. During the two waves of Viking raids, contact with Rome had become more spasmodic than before, but between them, during the tenth century, it had resumed its previous regularity. Alfred's successors had been hailed by the Vatican as Christian kings; Edgar in particular had played a prominent part in the monastic revival headed by the three great monastic saints, Dunstan, Oswald and Æthelwold, and had founded many monasteries. But Edgar's death and the second wave of

Viking raids ended this, and by the time Edward succeeded to the throne, the English Church was still recovering the energy it had lost during half a century of war and turmoil. Unfortunately, this coincided with the beginning of the reform movement in the Vatican in the 1040s, and by 1066 this was in full flood.

Under normal circumstances, the urgency of the Vatican to raise ecclesiastical standards, to stamp out simony and plurality, and to enforce a celibate clergy, and the slightly exhausted state of the English Church could have been reconciled over time. England was not the only Christian state that found difficulty in accepting immediately the new principles such as the celibacy of the clergy that were being formulated in Rome, and the papacy itself was not immaculate by the new standards; many of the highest ranking clergy there held in plurality. The situation in England was complicated by one particular problem: the status of the Archbishop of Canterbury.

As we have seen, when Robert of Jumièges, appointed and consecrated archbishop in 1051, fled in 1052, Stigand, then Bishop of Winchester, was appointed in his place without reference to Rome. Since Robert had never been canonically removed, this, in the eyes of the Pope, constituted an illegal intrusion, and Stigand was never recognised by the Vatican as validly appointed, and was never accorded the pallium[lxxv] by which the Pope conferred his authority on archbishops. Stigand survived the conquest and, indeed, the first few years of William's reign, the latter having presumably found him too useful to discard immediately; but he was deposed at a legatine council in 1070, on grounds that included the accusations that he had retained his bishopric of Winchester and thus held in plurality and that he had been summoned and excommunicated by four Popes. It is true that Stigand's relations with Rome had caused problems and that, while he was archbishop, no English bishop had accepted consecration at his hands except for one, who later pleaded rather improbably that he did not know that Stigand was under interdict. Harold had clearly taken care that his new church at Waltham should not be consecrated by Stigand, and, if Florence of Worcester is to be believed, Stigand did not crown him either. None the less, the accusations made against him in 1070 are hard to square with the facts that, in other respects, Stigand exercised his functions as archbishop normally from 1052 to 1070 and was in no way shunned by either clergy or laity, English or foreign. The papal envoys who visited the English Church in 1062 made no criticism of him although they did criticize Ealdred for holding the archbishopric of York and the bishopric of Worcester in plurality. Irregular as his position might be, it could hardly be compared, for example, with the scandal of the appointment of William's half-brother, Odo, to the bishopric of Bayeux at the uncanonically early age of thirteen. It seems, however, that, as far as Rome was concerned, Stigand's presence cast a taint over the whole English Church, and presented William and the reformers in the Vatican with a very convenient stick with which to beat the English. William of Poitiers takes pains to assure us that the duke's intention was 'not so much to increase his own power and glory as to reform Christian observance in those regions'.

When Gilbert of Lisieux arrived in Rome in 1066, therefore, he had a very strong case to present. His master had been promised the succession by the recently deceased king, Harold had sworn to uphold his claim and was now forsworn and perjured by usurping the crown himself; and, most persuasively, Vatican support in placing William on the throne that was his due would be repaid by a cleansing of the Augean stables of the English

Church by a man who had proved himself effective in implementing every aspect of the papal reform agenda in Normandy. No record of the council in which he presented his case has survived; all that is known is that there was no English presence to represent the other side, and, as far as we know, no request was made for an English reply to the allegations made by Gilbert. There was, of course, no reason why there should have been a reply; the election of the king of the English was a matter for the English alone and had never been subject to Vatican approval. The only clue we have is a letter written many years later to William by Hildebrand, by then Pope Gregory VII, that indicates fairly clearly the part he had taken in the proceedings and places it in the context of the Hildebrandine policy of attempting to persuade the temporal rulers of Christendom to swear fealty to the Holy See. His letter was the preliminary to his making his demand for fealty to William (which in fact came the following month – and was refused). On 24 April 1080, he wrote:

> I believe it is known to you, most excellent son, how
> great was the love I ever bore you, even before I
> ascended the papal throne, and how active I have shown
> myself in your affairs; above all how diligently I
> laboured for your advancement to royal rank. In
> consequence I suffered dire calumny through certain
> brethren insinuating that by such partisanship I gave
> sanction for the perpetration of great slaughter. But God
> was witness to my conscience that I did so with a right
> mind, trusting in God's grace and, not in vain, in the
> virtues you possessed.[lxxvi]

The man who later in the same letter expressed the Church's policy in the words, 'Cursed be the man that keepeth back his sword from blood' was certainly not the man to have been distressed by the carnage of Hastings. The promise of root and branch ecclesiastical reform in England was a cause in which Hildebrand would have regarded any amount of bloodshed as justifiable, impelled, as he says he was, by his conviction that it was his duty 'to cry aloud and spare not'; but if it had not been for the low esteem in which the English Church was then held in Rome and, in particular, the scandal of Stigand's situation, it is doubtful whether even he could have persuaded his brethren to support the unprovoked invasion of a peaceful and law-abiding nation, close for many centuries to the Vatican, by a foreign adventurer in search of a crown. As it was, the Hildebrandine arguments ultimately prevailed, William was apparently sent, along with the blessing of Pope Alexander II, a papal banner as witness to the justice of his cause, and the invasion took on the complexion of a holy war. It was, in words that have since been used to describe the first Crusade, 'a monstrous exercise in hypocrisy in which the religious motive [was] used merely as the thinnest of disguises for unashamed imperialism'.[lxxvii] With his objectives achieved, William only had to complete his preparations and wait for a suitable wind. After waiting long for this, as William of Poitiers tells us, he transferred his forces to St Valéry, either to take advantage of a shorter crossing to England or, according to William of Poitiers, blown there by a prevailing west wind.

There is, however, an alternative scenario. The whole business of William's appeal to the Pope rests on the unsupported evidence of William of Poitiers. Catherine Morton has examined the evidence for the episode and rejects it for a variety of reasons, among them that no other contemporary chronicler mentions it, that there was no more wrong with the state of the English Church than with the Norman, that the Pope's own legates had sat in council with Stigand in 1062 without complaint, and that the Normans of southern Italy were unlikely to concern themselves particularly with the diplomatic niceties of their former duke's proposed activities.[lxxviii] Primarily, she rejects it on the grounds that William of Poitiers was demonstrably a liar who did not even take the trouble to make his lies fit together. Harold's biographer, therefore, on the basis of Morton's research and a realistic assessment of the probabilities, suspects that no papal support was in fact provided for William's invasion. He points out that William of Jumièges, the only other contemporary Norman chronicler of William's deeds, makes no mention of any such support for William, which would be a curious omission for a churchman if it had been made public – and the duke would have had to make it public to benefit from it in recruiting. He guesses that what William of Poitiers describes in his account is 'a later retrospective sanction by the Papal court for the *fait accompli* represented by William's conquest'.[lxxix] This solution would clarify a lot of matters. Papal legates were sent to England in 1070, and it was as a result of their visit that Stigand was formally deposed, William was crowned (again) and a penance was imposed by Bishop Ermenfrid (who was one of the legates) on the Normans (not the English) who had fought at Hastings and had killed Englishmen after it. This would be very strange if the battle had been fought with papal sanction. It can only be explained by the assumption that William's invasion was not seen by the Vatican as a just war but, even in 1070, as one of aggression, though one that by that time it was obliged to accept and ratify.

This explanation of a retrospective sanction would explain the events of 1070 very convincingly; not only the penance imposed on the Norman troops by the papal legates, but also the second coronation of William during their visit (surely unnecessary after his coronation by Ealdred in Westminster Abbey in 1066 except as a papal endorsement of a *fait accompli*). It is tempting also to see this legatine council as the cause of William's foundation of Battle Abbey on the site of the English defence, as his own personal part of the Norman penance.[lxxx] Battle Abbey was not completed and dedicated until 1094; the legend, originated and maintained by the monks of Battle that William had vowed a monastery on the site of the battle before it had ever taken place, has now been demolished. The council, in short, could be seen as a general ratification of the fact of conquest and clearing up of unfinished business.

Given the absence of any other corroborating documentation in the Vatican than Hildebrand's letter, the whole truth will probably never be known. Most historians of the period have accepted the fact that the duke's appeal to the Pope was made, and that the papal blessing and a papal banner were given. Although William of Poitiers states that the banner was carried before the duke during the battle, nothing that could possibly be interpreted as a banner of such significance can be identified on the Bayeux Tapestry, which would seem strange if, as is generally assumed, the Tapestry was commissioned by Odo, Bishop of Bayeux. There is the corroborating fact that Pope Alexander is known to have bestowed such a banner on Roger de Hauteville, younger brother of Robert Guiscard, together with absolution for all who fought with him against the heathen of Sicily.

The truth of the story of the banner, like that of the papal blessing, has usually been accepted by subsequent historians and is now part of the fable of the conquest. There may or may not have been such a banner. There may, or may not have been papal sanction of the conquest. On the other hand, it is difficult to make sense of Hildebrand's letter of 1080 to William except on the assumption that some very categorical sign of approval and blessing had been sent by the Pope in 1066 at the urging of Hildebrand, and that both Hildebrand and William were aware of the fact. The balance of probability is that there must have been some expression of support from the Vatican, from the Pope or possibly just from Hildebrand (which would not preclude the necessity for a regularization of the situation in 1070), but it is fair to point out the arguments against this conclusion.

In the meantime, in England, Tostig had made his first contribution to the English defeat. The preliminary skirmish in May had convinced Harold that his brother was acting in league with William and that his descent upon the south coast was the preliminary to the full-scale invasion he was expecting. He called out the fyrd, and mobilized the navy. On this occasion he may well have called out the general fyrd, for the Chronicle tells us that he gathered a greater land and ship army than any king had ever raised before, but it telescopes events here, for it passes straight on from this remark to events later in the year. Florence of Worcester gives a fuller account:

> King Harold arrived at Sandwich and waited there for
> his fleet. When it was assembled, he crossed over with it
> to the Isle of Wight, and, inasmuch as William, count of
> the Normans, was preparing to invade England with an
> army, he watched all the summer and autumn for his
> coming. In addition he distributed a land force at
> suitable points along the sea-coast. But about the feast of

the Nativity of St Mary [8 September] provisions fell
short so that the naval and land forces returned home.[lxxxi]

These dates indicate that he had held the fyrd in service not for
the statutory two months but for nearly four, including the period
of harvest, so it is hardly surprising that provisions should have
run out. If William held his men together at Dives and St Valéry
without foraging, he did well, but it can only have been for about
half the time (though we have no certain knowledge of the date
when William assembled his army, the evidence points to this
being in early August). With hindsight, Harold must have been
aware that he had called out the fyrd too soon but his belief that
Tostig and William were acting in concert was reasonable; given
the time it took for the host to assemble, he dared not wait. The
land fyrd went home to rescue the harvest, the fleet was sent
around to London to refit. There are rumours (as has already been
noted, though the E Chronicle puts it earlier than September),
though no firm corroboration, that there was a sea encounter with
the Normans; if there was, it might have taken place at about this
time, perhaps coinciding with William's transfer of his forces from
Dives to St Valéry. It is known from the Norman sources that
there were storms in the Channel at this date, in which William
lost many men and ships; it is perfectly possible either that the
English fleet was also damaged in the storms (it is recorded that
some of Harold's ships were lost on the way to the North
Foreland), or that there was in fact an encounter between the two
opposing navies in which both sides lost ships as both were moving
east up the Channel. There is an interesting note in the Domesday
Book of a certain Æthelric of Kelveden in Essex who 'went away
to a naval battle against King William' and fell ill on his return.[lxxxii]
The storms at this point give some support to Harold's reasons

for standing his forces down. By the beginning of September, the period of the equinoctial gales had arrived, and normally seafaring would stop for the winter. The likelihood of William launching an attack later than this must have seemed to him to be much reduced. In fact, William's luck held and 1066 was to produce a St Martin's summer.

The reasons for William's move from Dives to St Valéry are controversial. Some historians think he was looking for a base closer to England, or that his army had exhausted the area around Dives. William of Poitiers, who normally misses no opportunity to attribute any event, however unfavourably it may have turned out, to the duke's foresight and sagacity, ascribes no such motive to the move:

> Presently the whole fleet, equipped with such great foresight, was blown from the mouth of the Dives and the neighbouring ports, where they had long waited for a south wind to carry them across, and was driven by the breath of the west wind to moorings at Saint-Valéry. There too the leader, whom neither the delay and the contrary wind nor the terrible shipwrecks nor the craven flight of many who had pledged their faith to him could shake committed himself. . .to the protection of heaven.[lxxxiii]

This does not imply any kind of strategic planning. It is much more probable that the duke left Dives with a wind that he thought would carry him to England but that veered, and instead found himself driven by storms that he could not resist up the Channel, finding no shelter until his ships reached St Valéry. It is clear from William of Poitiers that the losses he sustained in men, ships and morale were heavy, and that he had the dead who came ashore buried in secret in order that morale should not be lowered further. We do not know the exact date of this move, but can work it out backwards (approximately at least) from the fact that the *Carmen de Hartingae Proelis* tells us that he lay for about a fortnight at St Valéry before he could sail, which would imply a move just about the time that Harold stood down his troops and sent his fleet to London. It is possible that his spies had told him that Harold's force would have to be disbanded about this time, and that he had seized on this as the most opportune moment to make his attack and also probably the latest practicable time to do so before seafaring closed down for the winter. Although not a seaman himself, he would have had plenty of advisers to tell him when the Channel normally ceased to be navigable. If he had indeed succeeded in crossing the Channel at this time, he would have found Harold still in the south and (on the evidence of his later showing) well able to assemble a strong enough army to meet him successfully. What difference that encounter would have made to later events in the north can never be known.

We have to assume that both William and Harold had good intelligence systems set up and were both getting regular news of what went on on the other side of the Channel. Indeed, William of Poitiers tells that the duke captured one of Harold's spies, showed him around his camp and sent him home to tell his master what he had seen. With so many Normans settled in England, the duke had good opportunities of knowing what was going on there. Not only did the abbey of Fécamp hold extensive estates in Sussex (its estate at Steyning had been repossessed by Harold but it had retained its other estates at Rye), but also the very considerable benefice at Bosham (which had excellent access to the sea – Harold had sailed from there on his ill-fated visit to

Normandy) had been given by King Edward to his Norman chaplain, Osbern, later Bishop of Exeter, who was not only a cousin of William but whose brother was one of the duke's closest advisers. If Harold had been truly as calculating or as ruthless as the enemy he was preparing to repel, he would surely have expelled such Norman settlements as these from England as soon as he was crowned. On the other hand, he may have calculated that William was most likely to make for the part of England where he had assured allies, and it would have been helpful to a man who had the whole south coast to guard to have some idea where his enemy was most likely to land. If this was his calculation, it was correct. William did make for Sussex. With his intelligence network already installed, he would have known when Harold called out the fyrd. Perhaps it was not simply opposing winds that delayed his crossing but also the desire to keep his enemy guessing, the hope that Harold would eventually have to do what indeed he did do, disband his forces. In fact, if this was indeed his strategy, he could not have delayed much longer, and he very nearly left it too late. He could not have known, any more than Harold did, that there would be a period of prolonged summer in September and October; and indeed, he ran into the September equinoctial gales when many of his ships and men were lost on the voyage to St Valéry and then was obliged to wait with considerable anxiety for much longer than he wanted for a favourable wind. What we do not know is how much William knew of what was happening in the north of England.

Snorre Sturlason's *King Harald's Saga* claims that Tostig went in person to Norway before he appeared in May off the south coast of England. If he went to Sweyn Estrithson in Denmark, he might well have carried on to Norway. Snorre provides an account of his interview with Harald Hardrada. Tostig would, Snorre suggests, have reminded Harald of his own claim to the English throne through his nephew, King Magnus, and of the plunder to be expected in England; he would have suggested that, if they were to conquer England together, they could share the kingdom and its riches (he might, however, have reflected that, on past performance, Harald Hardrada was not a man likely to share a kingdom); and, possibly most persuasive of all his arguments, he would have pointed out that in York, the capital of the northern Danelaw, there would be much sympathy and support for an invader of Scandinavian origins. How far this was true is not easy to estimate now. We have seen that, when the Northumbrians rebelled in 1065 against their last earl, Tostig, they did so not to gain Northumbrian independence but to secure a non-Scandinavian replacement for him. What Tostig would have ignored in his anxiety to be reinstated in his earldom, and what he would naturally not have mentioned to Harald Hardrada, was his own great unpopularity in Northumbria generally and York in particular.

Whether or not Tostig went to Norway, whether or not Snorre's hypothetical conversation ever took place, contact must have been made between him and Hardrada in some way. Tostig, as we have seen, retired to Scotland to lick his wounds under the protection of King Malcolm and wait for the rendezvous. Snorre is irritatingly economical with dates, but says that Harald sailed from the Solund Isles to Shetland, where he stopped only briefly, before continuing to the Orkneys which were then Norwegian territory. Here he paused to deposit one of his two wives and both his daughters, and to pick up the Orcadian earls Paul and Erland with their men and ships. It has been estimated that, with what forces Tostig had been able to recruit from Scotland, the Norwegian armada consisted of about three hundred ships and nine thousand men. There may well have been more men than that. The crew of a Scandinavian warship could be anything between forty and eighty men, and, allowing for the fact that some of the ships would be supply ships that would hold fewer and whose crew might not be fighting men, it is not impossible that Hardrada's fighting force could have been as many as twelve thousand. He then sailed down the east coast of Scotland and England as far as Scarborough. When and where the junction with Tostig took place is uncertain. He may have picked him up off the Firth of Forth on his way south; Snorre says they did not meet until Hardrada arrived in England and that Tostig then became his man. We do not know, therefore, whether they were together when Hardrada sacked and subjugated Cleveland and Scarborough and burned the town. At Holderness an English force opposed him but was defeated. The Norwegian fleet then turned into the Humber and proceeded up it and up the Ouse as far as Riccall, driving before it Earl Morcar's ships, which were bottled up there at Tadcaster on the Wharfe, which joins the Ouse just above Riccall. Hardrada could have continued up the Ouse as far as York itself, but would then have risked the English ships coming back down river into the Ouse to cut off his retreat. At Riccall, he was only ten miles south of York.

From Riccall, leaving a substantial body of men to guard the ships, Hardrada and Tostig marched on York on 20 September but were confronted by Earls Edwin and Morcar at Gate Fulford, barring his road to the city. The English earls had thus had the opportunity to pick their ground for battle, and had arranged themselves with their right flank on the bank of the Ouse and their left defended by a deep ditch beyond which was bog and marshland. Hardrada, facing them, also drew up his army with one flank reaching down to the river Ouse, and the other and weaker stretching inland towards the dyke and the large area of swampy ground. He placed himself towards the river end where his forces were strongest, with his menacing standard Land Waster (a white silk banner on which Odin's bird, the black raven, gaped for slaughter with wings spread) over his head. According to Snorre, the English approached in close formation, and launched their first attack on the weaker wing opposing them. This almost immediately gave way and, as the English pursued them, Hardrada swung his stronger wing around to take them in the rear and the flank, pushing them into the boggy land. There was really no contest. The English fought well but when pushed back into the quagmire behind them, many took flight and were drowned either in the river or in the swamp – so many, in fact, that it was said that the Norwegians could cross the swamp dry-shod on the bodies of the dead. Edwin and Morcar survived, and surrendered York on 24 September. They could hardly do anything else. The fact that the city was not sacked may have been because it was the capital of Tostig's old earldom and he wanted it back. None the less, the fate of Scarborough, if known to the citizens, would have done much to persuade them to accept whatever terms were offered.

Hardrada demanded hostages from all the main Northumbrian families, helpfully identified for him by Tostig, provisions for his army and agreement that the Northumbrians would join with his forces and march south to conquer the rest of England. According to Florence of Worcester, Hardrada also gave hostages in return; if so, this was presumably in earnest of his future good faith if he conquered England and a gesture to ingratiate himself with the men of York. This is not confirmed in any of the surviving versions of the Anglo-Saxon Chronicle, which merely say that Hardrada took hostages. Some of these were delivered immediately, but more, and much of the commissariat, had to come from a distance. Since York was inadequately supplied to maintain the Norwegian army, Hardrada withdrew to his ships to await deliveries, which it was agreed should take place on 25 September at Stamford Bridge on the Derwent, a convenient central and strategic point where several roads met.

Since he had stood down the fyrd in the first fortnight of September, King Harold must have been waiting with considerable apprehension to see which of the two invasions would come first. The speed with which he reacted to both suggests that he had already arranged some early-warning system, but he could hardly have heard of Hardrada's landing earlier than the attack on Scarborough, and even then he may not have been certain to begin with whether it was a full-scale invasion or merely a raiding party. As soon as the gravity of the situation – too grave for the young and untried northern earls to deal with by themselves – became clear, he was faced with the alternatives of leaving the south coast undefended while he attended to the northern invasion or staying where he was, on guard for the Normans. This would have given Hardrada and Tostig, already on the spot, the opportunity to strengthen their position in a notoriously turbulent part of the country. King Harold must have been aware that the wind had been settled northerly for the past few weeks, perfect for bringing the Norwegians, impossible for the Normans. It may have seemed a worthwhile venture to march north, face Hardrada and hope to get back to the south coast before the wind changed, and he opted for it. He may have left part of his forces in the south with a watching brief; he probably resummoned the fyrd before he left. On the assumption that he might have had the news from the north at any time between 18 and 20 September, he probably left London with his housecarls and whatever other forces he could take not later than the 20th on a day and night march that brought him to Tadcaster on 24 September, an incredible feat of speed. Twenty miles was normally considered a good day's march; the distance from London to York is about two hundred miles. To have reached Stamford Bridge in fighting order by early morning on the 25th, the English must have done between forty and fifty miles a day. At Tadcaster, according to the Chronicle, he paused to array his fleet, presumably the ships that Hardrada had bottled up there. The word *lið* that the Chronicle uses normally means a fleet, but it is also used occasionally for land forces and for the men who would have fought on the ships, and in this case it would make much better sense to understand it as arraying his army, which he would have supplemented with levies on his way north and with the men from the fleet. He would also have heard, on arrival or en route, of the result of the battle of Fulford and that the Norwegians were even then awaiting the delivery of hostages and provisions at Stamford Bridge. On the 25th, he marched for York, where he would have picked up Edwin and Morcar with the remnants of their men (if they were still fit for service), and passed straight through the city for Stamford Bridge. R. Allen Brown sees in the surrender of the citizens of York to Hardrada a confirmation of Northumbrian separatism at this time and a lack of enthusiasm for the rule of Harold Godwinson, the brother of Earl Tostig whom they had so recently thrown out;^{lxxxiv} in that case, it is remarkable that no citizen of York slipped out of the city ahead of the English army to give warning of its advance. According to Snorre, Harold closed all the city gates to make sure that no warning was given. It is not known where Snorre got this information; it is not corroborated in any English accounts, but these are so sparse on the subject of Stamford Bridge that this cannot of itself be held to disprove Snorre's assertion. At all events, no warning was given. On this occasion, the St Martin's summer operated in Harold's favour. Hardrada, Tostig and about two-thirds of their men were lounging by the river, waiting for the hostages and supplies. It was a hot day and the men had left their mail coats and much of their armour at the ships. In Snorre's words,

> The weather was exceptionally fine, with warm
> sunshine; so the troops left their armour behind and
> went ashore with only their shields, helmets, and spears,
> and girt with swords. A number of them also had bows
> and arrows. They were all feeling very carefree.[lxxxv]

When they saw the cloud of dust raised by the approaching army coming over the brow of the hill, they were at first uncertain what it portended; then, 'the closer the army came, the greater it grew, and their glittering weapons sparkled like a field of broken ice'.[lxxxvi] Tostig advised retreating to their ships and making a stand there, although the approach of the English host blocked the quickest way back to them; Hardrada compromised by sending his best riders to summon the rest of his army, and formed up his men into a shield wall with the wings curved so far back that it was almost circular, with his Land Waster standard in the centre.

The battle of Stamford Bridge, no less than the battle of Hastings, is encrusted with legends, and it is difficult to tell which legend originated at which battle. Hardrada, like William, fell before the battle when his horse stumbled, and claimed that a fall was good luck. King Harald Hardrada, like King Harold Godwinson, is said to have died from an arrow shot. The exchanges before the battle may have a foundation in reality, or may not. Snorre is a late witness:

Twenty horsemen from the English king's company of Housecarls came riding up to the Norwegian lines; they were all wearing coats of mail, and so were their horses.

One of the riders said, 'Is Earl Tostig here in this army?'

Tostig replied, 'There is no denying it – you can find him here.'

Another of the riders said, 'Your brother King Harold sends you his greetings, and this message to say you can have peace and the whole of Northumbria as well. Rather than have you refuse to join him, he is prepared to give you one third of all his kingdom.'

The earl answered, 'This is very different from all the hostility and humiliation he offered me last winter. If this offer had been made then, many a man who is now dead would still be alive, and England would now be in better state. But if I accept this offer now, what will he offer King Harald Sigurdsson for all his effort?'

The rider said, 'King Harold has already declared how much of England he is prepared to grant him: seven feet of ground, or as much more as he is taller than other men.'

Earl Tostig said, 'Go now and tell King Harold to make ready for battle. The Norwegians will never be able to say that Earl Tostig abandoned King Harald Sigurdsson to join his enemies when he came west to fight in England. We are united in our aim: either to die with honour, or else conquer England.'

The horsemen now rode back.

Then King Harald Sigurdsson asked, 'Who was that man who spoke so well?'

'That was King Harold Godwinsson,' replied Tostig.

King Harald Sigurdsson said, 'I should have been told much sooner. These men came so close to our lines that this Harold should not have lived to tell of the deaths of our men.'

'It is quite true, sire,' said Earl Tostig, 'that the king acted unwarily, and what you say could well have happened. But I realized that he wanted to offer me my life and great dominions, and I would have been his murderer if I had revealed his identity. I would rather that he were my killer than I his.'

King Harald Sigurdsson said to his men, 'What a little man that was; but he stood proudly in his stirrups.'[lxxxvii]

We may be on safer ground with the legend of the Norwegian warrior who single-handed held the bridge across the Derwent while the Norwegian army drew itself up on the far side, and could only be killed by one of the English who took a boat under the bridge and stabbed him through the gaps between the planks. It is reported at the end of the C version of the Chronicle, though the entry is clearly a late addition in language a good hundred years later than the rest of the entry; but it is strange that Snorre should not have included a deed of Norse heroism if the story of it had been taken back to Norway.

Once the bridge was clear, the English were able to attack. According to Snorre, they opened with a cavalry charge, and this has been seized on as proof that the pre-conquest English did occasionally fight on horseback. But the lateness of this account and the many inaccuracies it contains make this a very doubtful proposition. The English, or some of them at least, may have ridden to the battlefield but would probably then have fought, as at Hastings, on foot. Hardrada's main preoccupation would have been to withstand the attack until reinforcements from his ships could arrive; Harold's would have been to make sure that he did not. Hardrada's curved shield wall was essentially a defensive position, but without their body armour his men were unusually vulnerable, and, in the hand-to-hand fighting that followed, they were cut down in hordes. The first phase of the battle ended when Hardrada turned berserker himself and rushed forward into the front of the battle. 'Neither helmets nor coats of mail could withstand him, and everyone in his path gave way before him.'[lxxxviii] At this point, according to Snorre, he was struck by an arrow in the throat and died.

The king's death, as so often in mediaeval warfare, caused a hiatus in the proceedings, and at this juncture, again according to Snorre, King Harold renewed his offer to his brother and quarter to all surviving Norwegians. The offer was rejected, and the fighting around Land Waster resumed. The third phase of the battle started when the Norwegians from the ships, led by Eystein Orri, arrived to reinforce Tostig. The odds were not as uneven as might be supposed: the Norwegians were, most of them, fighting without armour, but the English were fighting without sleep, after a heroic forced march of several days; both sides were by this time exhausted by the battle and the heat – indeed, Snorre reports that even those from the ships who did have armour threw it off, and that many died from heat exhaustion without striking a blow, after covering the miles from Riccall at top speed. The fighting continued until late in the afternoon, by which time Tostig had also fallen, and those who had survived the carnage fled back to the ships, pursued by the English. There is no evidence to show who was responsible for Tostig's death; Guy of

Amiens attributes it to Harold, but this was obviously so that he could add the label of fratricide to those of perjurer and usurper. It was reported that his body was so mutilated that it could only be identified by a wart between the shoulders, and it was given honourable burial in York after the battle. Hardrada's young son Olaf and the two Orcadian earls, who had all been with those who had remained with the ships, were given quarter and leave to return home by Harold, after swearing oaths never to attack England again, an oath that Olaf honoured when he succeeded his brother as king. Harold allowed them to take as many ships as were necessary for their remaining men. They took twenty-four, out of the three hundred that had brought them.

If it had not been for what happened so soon afterwards, Stamford Bridge would be remembered as a battle of the highest significance in its own right. The death of Harald Hardrada, the legendary and most feared warrior of his time, and the destruction of his army, marked the end of the Viking age that had influenced so much of Europe, from Byzantium to the Atlantic. It also marked the end of centuries of assault on England; although there were to be sporadic and local attacks thereafter, mainly from Sweyn Estrithson, there would be nothing on the scale of what had gone before. Under any circumstances, it was a remarkable achievement for the last Anglo-Saxon king of England, one that the bones of Alfred, Edward the Elder and Æthelred would have saluted; in the peculiar circumstances of 1066, it was astonishing. But it was not achieved without damage. The Norwegian army may have been virtually destroyed, but they took many Englishmen with them. Between the men lost by Edwin and Morcar at Gate Fulford and those killed and wounded at Stamford Bridge, the fighting strength of the kingdom was much diminished.

THE BATTLE

The battle of Stamford Bridge was fought on 25 September. On the day it was fought William was still at St Valéry, waiting for a favourable wind. The *Carmen de Hastingae Proelio,* a slightly controversial source, partly because of problems of dating and attribution, partly because clearly written for entertainment, takes up the story at this point and gives a harrowing picture of his anxiety:

> Here you had a long and troublesome delay, spending a
> fortnight in that territory waiting for succour from the
> Supreme Judge. You visited the Saint's church often,
> devoutly, with sighs and prayers making pure offerings to
> him. You looked to see by what wind the church's
> weathercock was turned. If it was from the south, you
> departed happily. But if, on a sudden, the North wind
> interrupted and held it at bay, tears streamed down your
> cheeks. You were forsaken. It was cold and wet and the
> sky was hidden by clouds and rain.[lxxxix]

William had gone so far as to cause the body of the saint to be removed from his tomb and carried around the town in procession to the accompaniment of prayers, to ensure, as William of Poitiers puts it, that the contrary wind became a favourable one. On the 28th, his prayers were answered. Christine and Gerald Grainge wrote an extremely interesting paper about the voyages from Dives to St Valéry and from St Valéry to Pevensey from the point of view of the sailor, in which they discuss the hazards William's mariners would have faced in sailing from St Valéry. According to them, a typical series of Atlantic low pressures in the Channel would have brought the weather that so distressed William; this was succeeded on the 28th by a high pressure system that brought with it warm weather, clear skies and a southerly wind. By their calculations, high tide at St Valéry on the 28th would have been at 1514 hours.[xc] Since the fleet would have been dependent on the ebb tide to get them out of harbour, embarkation must have been undertaken at breakneck speed. Both William of Poitiers and the *Carmen* tell us that, by the duke's orders, the fleet hove to once it had cleared the coast to enable the stragglers to catch up and the ships to assemble in some sort of order. William, however, also tells us that during the night the duke's ship so far outstripped the rest of the fleet that he found himself entirely alone at daybreak. Needless to say, he behaved, according to his chronicler, with the greatest sangfroid, eating breakfast on board as if he were in his chamber at home, while waiting for the rest of the ships to catch up with him. Had Harold still had his fleet patrolling off the Isle of Wight, the duke might have been in some danger, though it would have been very much a matter of luck if one isolated ship had been spotted by them. As it was, the Norman fleet landed at Pevensey at daybreak on the 29th, apart from a few ships that became separated from the main fleet and landed at Romney where the crews were attacked and slaughtered by the inhabitants.

It is a matter of conjecture whether William had any news of the Norwegian invasion before he sailed. With the winds in the north as they were before the 28th, it would not have been impossible for word to have been brought to him of the invasion; the knowledge that King Harold had marched north to repel it would certainly have been known to his intelligencers in the south. It is highly unlikely, however, that, even if he knew of the invasion, he could have heard of the result of Stamford Bridge and indeed it is fairly clear from William of Poitiers' account that he had not. He may have landed, not knowing whether he would have to face King Harold of England or King Harald of Norway; he may not have known about the latter's invasion at all; he may have been completely mystified to find a virtually undefended shore to greet him. He lost no time in profiting by the opportunity it presented. Having erected a wooden castle on the remains of the old Roman fortifications, he went out personally with some of his leaders to prospect. It took him very little time to realize that Pevensey (where he may have landed as much by chance as by choice), though a good harbour, was a poor base for freedom of movement, and to decide to transfer his headquarters to Hastings.

The coastline of the Pevensey and Hastings area has changed substantially since the eleventh century. Pevensey is no longer on the coast; then, it was at the head of a sizeable inland lagoon (which has since become Pevensey Levels), ideal for sheltering large numbers of ships, but unsuitable for the kind of manoeuvring that William had in mind. In order to move east, towards Hastings and the main road to London, he first had to proceed west to circumvent the large areas of salt marsh, with frequent tidal inlets, which his men could not march across. He could then have turned north-east towards Hastings, descending on it from not far south of where the battle was actually to be fought. At Hastings, which had been one of Alfred's fortified *burhs*, he would have found a harbour adequate for his ships and a good defensive position on what was then virtually a promontory, a triangle lying between the Brede estuary, the Bulverhythe estuary and the sea, with the only land exit the road to London. He would also have found the remains of the old Roman fortifications as well as those of Alfred's, an ideal site for another of his wooden castles. How much of Alfred's fortifications remained nearly two centuries after they were built is uncertain, but the earthen ramparts would almost definitely have survived. There is a certain irony in the fact that one of the strong points built by Alfred to defend his kingdom against Viking invaders should have served as the base for a latter-day pirate of Viking descent. Since time seemed to be on his side for the present, he would probably have had the horses ridden around the salt marshes to Hastings to avoid the risky business of another embarkation and disembarkation of them, while the ships sailed or were rowed around. Once comfortably established there, he could send out his men to ravage the surrounding lands (most of them belonging to the Godwin family) for provisions while he waited upon events.

The first of these, according to William of Poitiers, was the arrival of a messenger from Robert FitzWymark, a man of Norman or Breton parentage long settled in England, and related to both the duke and the former king – the Robert FitzWymark who less than a year previously had been present at the deathbed of Edward the Confessor. The message he sent to the duke was that

> King Harold has fought with his own brother and with
> the king of the Norwegians, who passed for the
> strongest man living under the sun, and has killed both

in one battle and destroyed huge armies. Encouraged by this success, he is advancing against you by forced marches, leading a strong and numerous troop; against him I consider that your men would be worth no more than so many wretched dogs. . . I urge you, stay behind fortifications.[xci]

William's reply was that he would fight Harold as soon as possible and had confidence in the ability of his men to destroy him 'even if I had only 10,000 men of the quality of the 60,000 I have brought with me'. He spoke with bravado; it is unlikely that he had more than the 10,000 he referred to so disparagingly. Whether because of FitzWymark's warning or native prudence, he did, however, stay within his fortifications, maintaining close contact with his ships, while he awaited Harold's arrival.

The situation in the north is much vaguer, since there was no chronicler to leave an account and no direct evidence of the sequence of events survives. It has been calculated that the earliest the king could have had news of the Norman landing was 1 October, which presupposes the arrangement of a relay network of mounted messengers between London and York. (Robert FitzWymark's warning to William illustrates well the efficiency of the intelligence the duke could rely on; for FitzWymark to get this information to him so fast, ahead of the king's arrival in London after an exceptionally rapid march, he must have set up his own system of relay messengers to bring the news.) In the days between the battle on the 25th and the arrival of the news from the south, there would have been more than enough to do in the north, with the despatch of the surviving Norwegians, the burial of the more distinguished English dead (Orderic Vitalis speaks decades later of the mountain of dead men's bones that still bore witness to the terrible slaughter on both sides), the tending of the wounded and the restoration of order in York itself.

The Chronicle does not say whether the news of the Norman landing reached the king in York or whether he had already started south and met it on the way. The balance of probability, supported by Florence of Worcester, is that he was still in York and set out for London immediately. If he left on the 2nd and maintained the same impressive speed he achieved on the journey north, he would have arrived in London on 6 or 7 October. On the other hand, he may have been slowed by wounds inflicted at Stamford Bridge on many of his crack troops; he may indeed have been wounded himself. He may have collected contingents of men on the way south who had not been in time to meet him on his march to York. Few things testify more convincingly to the efficiency of the English military organization (and, indeed, to Harold's general acceptance as king) than his ability to raise so many effective armies in so short a time between May and October. None the less it would have been the housecarls who bore the brunt of the Norwegian assault at Stamford Bridge, and even their legendary fighting capacity must have been weakened by it. According to some accounts, he diverted his march to offer prayers at Waltham Abbey, his own foundation, but this cannot greatly have delayed his arrival in London, where his first preoccupations would be to rest his men, send his fleet to cut off the Norman retreat and coordinate the levies that were coming in.

At this point, William of Poitiers takes up the story again. According to him, Harold sent an emissary to William, restating the right by which he held the throne and bidding William leave his kingdom with all his men. William replied at much greater length, setting out the basis of his own claim and offering to submit his case to either English or Norman law or to trial by personal combat. According to the chronicler, 'we wish to bring the tenor of the duke's own words (which we have diligently sought out) rather than our own composition to the notice of many' as proof of the justice of the Norman cause.[xcii] The wisdom and justice that he endeavoured to illustrate by the lengthy speech reported are not, in fact, very clearly demonstrated. By English law William had no case, there was no reason why the English succession should be determined by Norman law any more than by the Pope, and trial by combat had at this time no status in the English legal system and did not have until William at a later date altered that system to accommodate it. And, in parenthesis, if William's invasion had indeed been blessed by the Pope, it would have been most improper for him to have devalued that blessing by offering any of these alternatives. It is likely that the speech reported here by William of Poitiers, like the speech attributed to the duke at the beginning of the battle, was his own composition. On the other hand, such an exchange of embassies would have been a perfectly normal proceeding in such a situation. The main point of interest about this one is that, if it did take place, it makes nonsense of the claim made by both William of Poitiers and the *Carmen* that Harold's objective was to take William by surprise, as he had done with Hardrada. If you plan to take your enemy by surprise after a forced march of exceptional speed, you do not first of all send a formal embassy to him letting him know exactly where you are.

The question of what Harold's plans actually were now becomes important. William's situation was straightforward. The success of his venture depended entirely upon how soon he could gain an outright and crushing victory over his opponent. It has been suggested that the savage pillage and harrying of Harold's lands in Sussex had been designed in part at least to provoke Harold into confronting him as soon as possible. It is true that the obligations of mediaeval kingship dictated that Harold should avenge the slaughter of his people, more especially when they were the people of Sussex among whom he had grown up; but pillage and rapine on this scale was, as we have seen, a fairly routine act of war. It seems unlikely that a commander as experienced as Harold would allow himself to be provoked into precipitate action by it. He had, after all, done a good deal of harrying himself in the past. His situation was, in a way, as straightforward as William's. William needed a quick and decisive victory as soon as possible, preferably without moving so far from his base that his lines of communication with his ships could be cut; Harold presumably also desired a quick and decisive victory but he did not need it as urgently as William did. He had the luxury of a choice that William did not have. William had to win; Harold could afford a draw. He could retreat from the battlefield in order to regroup and reattack, as Alfred and Edmund Ironside had done on several such occasions.

More important than this, he had the option of not fighting a pitched battle at all. William could not have stayed bottled up on the Hastings peninsula for ever. By 14 October, he must have pretty well exhausted the provisions that could be provided by the surrounding country, and would have been unable to feed his men without moving further away from his base. By far the most sensible strategy for Harold would have been to draw William away from his ships into the interior of the country, over territory unknown to him that had preferably been stripped in advance of anything that could have offered sustenance to the Norman army. Famine, as Vegetius had said, is more terrible than the sword, and in this case could easily have been arranged. William's stragglers and foragers could have been cut off and destroyed, and the main part of his army could have been engaged and defeated with minimal loss to the English at whatever time seemed to offer the best advantage, when they had recovered from the stress of Stamford Bridge and two long forced marches, and had been supplemented by further levies. This was the kind of strategy that Harold had employed in the past against Gruffydd ap Llewellyn, and it is unbelievable that he did not resort to it again in 1066. The really interesting question is why.

Various explanations have been offered for Harold's tactics (or apparent lack of them) at this time. There were rumours after Hastings that he had been ill before Stamford Bridge, that he had had some sort of infection in his leg that made it impossible for him to ride. There are always such rumours after the event, impossible to verify later, but if this one is true, it makes his victory at Stamford Bridge even more remarkable. He may have been wounded at Stamford Bridge and he must, at the very least, have been exhausted by the time he reached Hastings, as must most of his army, a situation that contrasted cruelly with the well-rested and well-fed condition of the Normans who had spent a fortnight living comfortably off the fat of Harold's lands. By 1066 he was probably about forty-four, by the standards of the day no longer a young man. A paper written by a psychiatrist, Dr Max Sugar, endeavours to ascribe what he terms the king's loss of initiative and nerve before Hastings to a clinical depression brought on by his excommunication by the Pope and consequent conviction of the damnation of his soul. The idea that Harold had been excommunicated has been adopted by several writers and has muddied the historical waters. Setting aside the fact that there is at least a modicum of doubt whether the Pope was involved at all in William's invasion before it took place, there is absolutely no evidence that Harold was formally excommunicated (any more than William himself had been when he defied the Pope's prohibition on his marriage with Matilda of Flanders). If William was proclaiming his invasion a holy war (which he was), Harold would have known of it from his spies and would presumably have been extremely annoyed. But that would be a long way from excommunication.

The arguments in this paper, relying, as they too often do, on late or unreliable authorities, cannot be taken very seriously. None the less there are questions that have to be asked and are very difficult to answer. The Harold whom we see during the days between Stamford Bridge and Hastings seems not to be the Harold who is portrayed by the author of the *Vita Ædwardi* as 'passing with watchful mockery through all ambushes, as was his way.'[xciii] Why did he afford William the early battle that was so crucial to him and might be so disastrous to Harold himself? Why, when he was having heavy losses during the battle, did he not withdraw his forces into the forest behind him? Orderic, unsupported by William of Poitiers or indeed any other earlier source, says that Harold's younger brother, Gyrth, attempted to persuade him to allow him to lead the English army so that in case of disaster Harold would still be alive to lead the resistance against William. Gyrth's main argument was that he had sworn no oaths to William and could therefore defend his country with a clear conscience. This would have been a sensible proposal, but hardly practicable in the circumstances in which it was made. The first duty of any king at this time was to protect his kingdom and people. The main reason for Harold's unanimous election as king was his ability to defend the country. His reputation as a warrior was second to none in England, his opposition to a Norman takeover (or indeed a Norwegian one) was well known and of long standing. At Stamford Bridge he had triumphantly vindicated the trust put in him, and in the minds of most Englishmen at that time, Hardrada, because of his fearsome reputation, represented a much greater threat than the then comparatively unknown Norman duke; for Harold not to lead his forces in person against William, not to have revenged the outrages committed against his people, would have severely compromised his credibility as king and his ability to govern in future. Indeed, it is doubtful if such a stratagem would have worked. The army raised by Edmund Ironside against Cnut before his father's death in 1016 refused (apparently legally) to fight because his father, the king, was not with them. The fact that Æthelred must at this stage have been a dying man clearly made no difference. The custom presumably originated for the protection of a king against ambitious heirs and nobles. In 1016 it worked against the national interest. We shall never know how it would have worked in 1066. If, on the other hand, Gyrth also advised him to adopt delaying tactics and draw William away from the coast, as he is also reported to have done, he would have been on much surer ground.

The frequently offered explanation, that Harold hoped, in a fit of rashness and overconfidence, to repeat the strategy that had worked so well against Hardrada, is not really convincing. In the first place, if indeed emissaries were exchanged before the battle, he was obviously not counting on the element of surprise that had been crucial to his previous victory; and in the second, he must have known that the situation was totally different. The surprise attack that he was able to make so triumphantly on Hardrada depended on a number of fortuitous circumstances (the assignation at Stamford Bridge to receive hostages, the weather, the division of Hardrada's army) that he could not have known about until he reached Tadcaster and heard what had happened and how he could turn it to the English advantage. The one thing he must have been certain about was that he would not catch William in the same way. He had campaigned with him in Brittany, he must have been aware that he would not catch William off guard and certainly not with his army split in two. The notion that Harold's strategy was dictated by his determination to surprise William as he had surprised Hardrada has become one of the accepted myths of Hastings; but it is important to remember that it originated solely in the brains of two Normans, William of Jumièges and William of Poitiers, neither of whom could possibly have known what the king was actually thinking or planning. There is no hint of any such design in the English sources. Haste, yes; surprise, no.

In one sense, Harold's experience of William's conduct of war in Brittany in 1064 may have been misleading. John Gillingham suggests that it was.

> Perhaps if Harold had witnessed William's sudden strike against Alençon in 1051 he might have been more on his guard in 1066. As it was, however, what he saw was a very typical example of William at war – a campaign in which the duke seems to have been prudently content with a small gain. . . In 1064 there was no sign of an aggressive, battle-seeking strategy. On the contrary it was a struggle of attrition in which, more than anything else, questions of supply seemed to dominate the course of events, a campaign very much in the style of all the other campaigns of the last fifteen years – a good guide, Harold might have thought in the summer of 1066, to the kind of war he was facing now.[xciv]

If he thought this, he might well have considered that a defensive, bottling-up strategy on his side would be the most effective and the least wasteful of his own men. But he might more prudently have reflected that William's very act in invading indicated an aggressive, battle-seeking strategy.

It is helpful at this point to look at the various accounts of the battle in the different sources, and the reasons given or implied for Harold's defeat, bearing in mind that none is written by an eyewitness and that all date from well after the event and share the benefit of hindsight. William of Jumièges gives no explanation and the briefest of accounts. William of Poitiers and the *Carmen de Hastingae Proelio*, as we have seen, ascribe it to Harold's overweening pride in thinking that he could take William by surprise, and Orderic Vitalis adopts this version from William of Poitiers. Of the English sources, which are more interesting in this context, the Chronicle (D) says that

> William came against him by surprise before his army
> was drawn up in battle array. But the king nevertheless
> fought bravely against him, with the men who would
> remain with him, and there were heavy casualties on
> both sides.

The E text says that Harold fought 'before all the army had come'. Florence of Worcester is more expansive: he says that although Harold

> well knew that some of the bravest Englishmen had
> fallen in the two former battles, and that one-half of his
> army had not yet arrived, he did not hesitate to advance
> with all speed into Sussex against his enemies. On

Saturday. . .before a third of his army was in order for fighting, he joined battle with them. . . But inasmuch as the English were drawn up in a narrow place, many retired from the ranks, and very few remained true to him. Nevertheless from the third hour of the day until dusk he bravely withstood the enemy, and fought so valiantly and stubbornly in his own defence that the enemy's forces could make hardly any impression.[xcv]

The Waltham Chronicle (the authors of which may even have had an eyewitness to help them since there is a legend that two of the canons of Waltham followed the English army to the battlefield) follow the E Chronicle and Florence of Worcester, lamenting that

the king who was the glory of the realm, the darling of the clergy, the strength of his soldiers, the shield of the defenceless, the support of the distressed, the protector of the weak, the consolation of the desolate, the restorer of the destitute, and the pearl of princes, was slain by his fierce foe. He could not fight an equal contest for, accompanied by only a small force, he faced an army four times as large as his.[xcvi]

What these accounts boil down to is that a) William took Harold by surprise, before his men were drawn up in battle array, b) Harold fought on a sit too constricted for his numbers, c) Harold fought too precipitately, before most of his men had arrived, and was outnumbered, and d) there were desertions. There are problems with these explanations, some of which are mutually contradictory and all of which, indeed, are the sort of accusations that tend to be levelled at commanders after a defeat. It is unlikely that he was outnumbered, though it must certainly have been true that his strength had been weakened by the events of the previous fortnight; his housecarls, who were reputed each to be as strong as two ordinary soldiers, must have stood the main brunt of the fighting at Stamford Bridge and many must have fallen. In numerical terms, it seems that the two armies were fairly evenly matched, and this is supported by the unusual length of the battle – eight to nine hours – arguing two forces very close in size, neither of which had a clear superiority over the other. We do not know what Florence of Worcester meant by 'one half of his army': half the full force that technically he could have called out (which could have been 40,000 men or more); or did he mean half of the levies whom he had actually summoned? Or half the force that he took to Stamford Bridge, many of whom may have been unfit for further service? If he had waited to fight, he could undoubtedly have had more men. On the other hand, if he had waited to fight, he might not have needed them.

However, the charge that William came on Harold before his men were properly arrayed does not make much sense. Harold is thought to have left London on 11 October on the sixty-mile march to the battlefield, reaching it in the evening of 13 October; if he left on the 12th, it does not affect the timetable much, it merely means that he and his men would have had less rest. He would have bivouacked overnight before the battle at the rendezvous he had appointed, the hoar apple tree, and formed up at daybreak on the 14th on the site he had chosen. According to William of Poitiers, the duke was told of Harold's approach by his scouts on the 13th (which in itself implies a departure from London on the 11th) and hastily ordered all those in the camp to arm themselves (for, says the chronicler, a great many of his men had been sent out foraging). According to William of Jumièges, the duke was so worried about the possibility of a surprise attack (which may be why William of Poitiers got the idea that Harold intended one) that he kept his men under arms all night just in case. What is not clear from any of the chronicles is whether he started from his camp at Hastings to meet Harold (who would be advancing by the London road) on the morning of the 14th or whether he marched at least part of the way to the battlefield the previous night. If the former, it has been estimated that he would have started his six-mile march from Hastings at approximately 6 a.m. on 14 October, which would have been first light, and that the head of his column would have reached the battlefield at about 8 a.m. If the latter, he could, of course, have been there earlier. Since there is no certain information, this is another occasion when we have to guess. It seems improbable, however, that he would have started his march to meet Harold while large numbers of his men were out foraging. But at this stage, it seems clear that the agenda was being set by Harold. He knew the country and had possibly already decided where to make his stand. It seems unlikely that William, given a free hand, would have chosen ground so unsuitable for cavalry.

The Battle Abbey Chronicle says that William halted his march at Hedgland (or Hecheland) where his troops put on their armour; this is a very late source, but it would have been a reasonable thing to do. He would not have wanted his men to arrive tired on the field from marching in armour. According to the Chronicle, it was while they were doing this that they got their first sight of the English; the Tapestry shows a scout arriving at that point to tell him of their position. According to the *Carmen,* William's forces were close enough to the battlefield, whether at Hedgland or further on, to see the English army emerge from the forest on to the ridge that was to be its fighting position and that blocked the road to London. It would therefore seem that both armies must have appeared virtually simultaneously on the field and deployed in full sight of each other. Harold cannot have been surprised by William's prompt arrival; he would have had his own scouts out, he knew where he was and would have been well aware how important it would be for William to offer battle as soon as possible. Indeed, if we are to credit William of Poitiers' version, William must, because of the uneven and marshy ground, have had to array his troops almost within stone's throw of the English line, since if he had done it earlier, they would have had to reform after they had negotiated the various impediments. This would normally have been considered an extremely hazardous proceeding since it would render him vulnerable to attack while his men were not in fighting order. He must have thought it safe on this occasion since it was highly unlikely that the English would desert the strong position they already occupied to attack or harass him while he was deploying, though it could have exposed his men to archery fire as they took up position; he could hardly have known at this stage that the king was short of archers. None of this, however, supports the idea that Harold had been caught unprepared, nor does the course of the battle thereafter suggest that the English suffered any disadvantage for such a reason. Indeed, William of Poitiers' account makes it clear that the English were fully prepared for the opening onslaught of the Norman archers and infantry.

As far as desertions are concerned, there are desertions in all battles, especially in a battle lasting so many hours, and on the losing side and after the leader is killed. If any rumour had been current that Harold had been excommunicated, this would certainly account for desertions, since no man was bound to fight for an excommunicated leader; but there is no evidence for that whatever. In the first place, it seems at least unlikely that there was any question of his having been formally excommunicated. Secondly, if he had been, William would certainly have made what capital he could out of the fact, and one would expect it to be referred to in Chronicle entries written after the battle, since it would support the idea, clearly widely prevalent, that the judgement of God had been given on William's side. It would have been a particularly appropriate justification of the usual formula, used by the Chronicle to record any English defeat from the wars of Alfred against the Danes onwards, that the Normans won 'as God granted it to them for the sins of the people' – or in this case the sins of the king. None the less it remains likely that there were desertions that cannot be ascribed to the king's death: the statement in the D Chronicle that the king fought bravely 'with the men who would remain with him', implies inescapably that there were some who would not, as does Florence of Worcester's statement that 'inasmuch as the English were drawn up in a narrow place, many retired from the ranks, and very few remained true to him'. William of Malmesbury's story that Harold refused to share out the Norwegian booty captured at Stamford Bridge among his men and placed it in the custody of Archbishop Ealdred until after the encounter with the Normans could offer another motive. If this were true (and William of Malmesbury is the only credible authority for the story, and a late one at that), it could indeed have caused some men to fall away from him and refuse to serve an ungrateful lord, even if the king had strategically a good reason for his refusal to distribute the loot immediately. No army marches fast or fights well when laden with booty, and he knew he would have to march fast and fight hard. The causes of the desertions can only be guessed at; the main point is that the entries in the English chronicles, especially the Anglo-Saxon Chronicle, would have been written by men who were as dependent as anyone else on reportage and hearsay after the event amid all the confusion of defeat. We cannot know how reliable their sources were.

A much more serious accusation is that Harold's choice of ground was poor. It was, in fact, peculiarly suitable for the kind of battle we must suppose him to have had in mind. It was so perfect that one can only suppose that, having been brought up in Sussex and knowing it as well as he did, he had picked it deliberately.

A longish watershed, roughly marked today by the course of Battle High Street, runs south, dipping slightly to a cross-ridge (rather like the head of a hammer). On either side of the watershed the ground fell away steeply; behind it to the north on Caldbec Hill was the site of the hoar apple tree, a distinctive local feature marking the boundaries of three different hundreds; behind that and all around was the primeval forest of Andredesweald. Such trees as this hoar apple frequently marked significant boundaries and were used as markers; they were easy places to appoint as a rendezvous for troops. The battle of Ashdown against the Danes in 871 was fought around an equally venerable thorn tree that was the meeting-place of the local hundred. The cross-ridge south of Harold's apple tree lay squarely across the London road. At its centre, the gradient was 1 in 15; at its west end, 1 in 33; at the east end, 1 in 22. At its foot, in front, was a brook, later dammed to form fishponds, presumably for the monks of Battle Abbey built by William after the battle, then presumably boggy, especially when pounded by cavalry for several hours. Indeed, as a result of the drainage of streams from the higher ground, both Caldbec Hill (on Harold's side of the field) and Telham Hill (on William's), much of the ground between the two armies seems to have been marshy and uncultivated.

It was along this cross-ridge, about eight hundred yards in length as far as one can tell today (the site has been altered by the building of the abbey), that Harold deployed his army. No surviving English chronicler tells us how he disposed of his men, but we know roughly where he set up his standards since the place was marked by the high altar of Battle Abbey, and it would have been on the slightly higher ground behind his front line, where he could see over his men's heads to the enemy lines. It was a superb defensive position. His main front, where the gradient was shallowest, would be occupied by the housecarls, his crack troops, with shire levies behind them, and the levies would presumably have defended the ends of the line where the declivity was steepest, possibly with a stiffening of housecarls and the Danish troops sent (according to William of Poitiers, probably accurate in this case) by his cousin, King Sweyn Estrithson. The normal English shield-wall formation was, in the words of Major-General J. F. C. Fuller, 'an essential one for infantry against cavalry relying on shock'[xcvii]. This was where he may have been influenced by his experience of the Norman cavalry when he had campaigned in Brittany. The shire levies are described in many accounts of the battle as unarmed peasants, equipped only with sticks and stones; there may have been many such present, burning to revenge the harrying the Normans had inflicted on them during the past fortnight, but the shire levies proper were, as we have seen, seasoned soldiers, mostly thegns or king's thegns, whose armour and equipment (as is testified by the Bayeux Tapestry) were virtually indistinguishable from that of the Norman infantry. It was no amateur army.

Harold seems to have sacrificed his archers, whom he had

certainly had at Stamford Bridge, in his rapid march south. If he had any, it is likely that the king would position them on his flanks where they would have the best chance of aiming at the charging enemy without wounding their own comrades, but this is guesswork only. In the absence of any documentary evidence, it must be assumed that they can have contributed little to their side of the battle. Under normal conditions, the Normans would have expected to reprovision themselves with the arrows shot by the enemy, but judging by William of Poitiers' emphasis on the hail of arrows in the later stages of the battle, they must have been adequately supplied by their own reserves.

Many writers have been convinced that Harold must have contemplated an attack at some stage, that he could never have intended a purely defensive action. It seems to me perfectly possible that he did just that. William was the aggressor, he was the defender. He must have been well aware that more men would join him as time went on; he certainly expected that the northern earls, his brothers-in-law, would be arriving with whatever forces they had remaining from Gate Fulford and Stamford Bridge (indeed, we know that they had got as far as London by the time the battle was fought); numerically, his position could only improve. William, on the other hand, as far as he knew, could not expect any reinforcements and if the English fleet could get around to Hastings to cut off his retreat, could be attacked from the rear as well. The duke was trapped in a small promontory of land, which he had already devastated with his customary thorough-ness, and would soon have been desperate for provisions. The only exits open to him were either to retreat to his ships and move further up or down the coast (a very risky manoeuvre, under his enemy's eye, and unlikely to succeed), or to advance by the London road, which was blocked by Harold. General Fuller believes that he would have been able to re-embark his men under cover of archery fire. We do not know how many archers William had, he seems to have had a lot, but, with all due respect to so senior and experienced an officer, it seems unlikely that archers, unsupported and, according to the Tapestry, mostly without body armour, could have withstood alone an attack by the full English army.

The corollary, of course, was that, like any animal at bay, he would attack at once. None the less, it may have seemed to Harold a perfectly feasible strategy to hold him in check and block his exit while his own position strengthened. The various chroniclers indicate that if he could have held his troops together and maintained his impregnable position, this would have been a reasonable tactic. If the situation had become dangerous, he could have withdrawn into the forest behind him to regroup and attack again on a more propitious occasion (allowing, it is true, that retreat along the narrow ridge behind him could have been a risky and slow manoeuvre). As has been pointed out, he did not need an outright victory at this point, he had everything to gain by luring William forward. In the meantime, by keeping him penned in where he was, he was at least preventing any further ravaging of the country. And if he could hold his ground until sunset, he would in effect have won. If William had had to withdraw to his bridgehead at Hastings at the end of the day without victory, with heavy losses, without provisions and with Harold still in possession of Caldbec Hill and the London road, he would have been in a very difficult situation. The only thing that prevented this from happening was Harold's death.

The insistence of so many historians on William's consummate generalship in this campaign has always seemed unaccountable. In the first place, he could have had no reason to expect so easy a landing in England, yet there is no evidence of any plan or preparation made by him for the contingency of his landing being strongly opposed other than his reported and prudent determination not to land in the dark. Even if he had known of Hardrada's and Tostig's invasion, he could have had no certainty when he sailed that the king would go north to oppose them, leaving the south shore undefended. There was no more than a 50:50 chance that he would do so. Again, even if he had known that Harold had gone, he does not appear to have had any plan of campaign for after his landing. He does not seem to have had any intention of securing strong points like Dover, Canterbury or even London while Harold was in the north. He established his bridgeheads at Pevensey and Hastings and waited. He might have waited in vain, and, as has already been pointed out, he could not have waited indefinitely. If Harold had been content to wait until hunger and low morale among the Norman troops had forced him to move inland, he would almost certainly have been defeated. He seems, in short, to have been in the position of a general who had managed to establish a bridgehead but had no plan of operation beyond it. Nothing but the incredible luck that attended him throughout the campaign saved him.

The one point on which there seems to be unanimity among the Norman chroniclers is the admission that, if the English had maintained their position on the ridge and had resisted the temptation to pursue the fleeing (or supposedly fleeing) enemy, it would have been virtually impossible to dislodge them. William of Poitiers speaks of 'one side attacking in different ways and the other standing firmly as if fixed to the ground'. Likewise the *Carmen* also speaks of the serried ranks of English standing as if rooted to the ground, and adds 'nor would the attackers have been able to penetrate the dense forest of the English had not invention reinforced their strength'. Baudri de Bourgeuil describes the

English as massed in a single dense formation, adding that they would have been impregnable if they had held together. Henry of Huntingdon writes that Harold had 'placed all his people very closely in a single line, constructing a sort of castle with them, so that they were impregnable to the Normans'. Wace condemns the English for having been lured by the feigned retreats into abandoning a position in which they could hardly have been defeated. Add to this the oral tradition that Harold had exhorted his troops before the battle not to be lured from their defensive position, and it will be seen that his tactics were not as foolish or short-sighted as has been suggested. They should have worked.

M. K. Lawson suggests that Harold's position was not confined to the ridge but may well have extended on his right flank to take in the hillock to the south-west of it; E. A. Freeman implies the same thing in his account of the battle. This hillock may be the mound depicted in plate 66 of the Bayeux Tapestry; the watercourse that the Tapestry shows as running close by it may have been the little stream that gave the battle its alternative name of 'Senlac' (*sand lacu* or sandy stream). He points out that there are serrations protruding from it that might indicate that it had been staked; if it had been, it would certainly have helped to bring down the horses that are portrayed as having fallen beside it. He supports the idea by reference to the *Carmen*, which describes the English position as comprising both a *mons,* which could describe the ridge, and a *vallis,* which could describe the declivity between the ridge and the hillock. It is an interesting theory, but not one that is easy to accept. In the first place, when would the English have had a chance to stake the water, if they only arrived exhausted late the previous evening (if indeed the serrations shown in the Tapestry are stakes. As Lawson says, they might just as well be reeds or foliage of some kind)? In the second, Harold would surely have been mad to put light-armed infantry (none of the English shown on the mound is wearing body armour) where they would have been unsupported by the housecarls and particularly vulnerable to the Norman cavalry. It is more likely that this plate shows the English who broke ranks to pursue the fleeing Bretons before taking refuge on the hillock and being cut down.

William would have had much less of a choice of ground and the site on which he did fight was particularly disadvantageous for the cavalry that were his greatest advantage over his enemy, since they would be obliged to charge uphill across what seems to have been very marshy and broken ground. His deployment is described by William of Poitiers, who is the best authority we have on the battle and who had the advantage of having served as one of William's knights before he took holy orders:

> He placed foot-soldiers in front, armed with arrows and
> cross-bows,[xcviii] likewise foot-soldiers in the second rank,
> but more powerful and wearing hauberks; finally the
> squadrons of mounted knights, in the middle of which
> he himself rode with the strongest force, so that he could
> direct operations on all sides with hand and voice.[xcix]

The *Carmen* supplements this information by saying that William positioned the Breton and other mercenaries on his left, the French and other mixed troops on his right, with the Normans led by himself in the centre, and this is corroborated to some extent by William of Poitiers who says a little later that the 'Breton knights and other auxiliaries on the left wing turned tail'. The *Carmen* opens the actual battle with what is probably the best known if most totally apocryphal story connected with it:

Meanwhile, with the result hanging in the balance and the bitter calamity of death by wounds still there, a juggler, whom a brave heart ennobled, putting himself in front of the duke's innumerable army, with his words encourages the French and terrifies the English, while he played by throwing his sword high in the air. When one Englishman saw a single knight, just one out of thousands, juggling with his sword and riding away, fired by the ardour of a true soldier and abandoning life, he dashed out to meet his death. The juggler, who was named Taillefer, when he was attacked spurred on his horse and pierced the Englishman's shield with his sharp lance. He then with his sword removed the head from the prostrate body, and turning to face his comrades, displayed this object of joy and showed that the opening move of the battle was his.

Strangely, the *Carmen* does not give the information that Taillefer rode towards the English singing the song of Roland; this detail is first supplied by Wace, never one to lose anything that would contribute to a good story. But it is William of Poitiers who gives by far the clearest and most convincing account of the actual fighting, as one would expect from a former soldier. It started ceremonially at 9 a.m. with the blare of trumpets from both sides, following which, by his account, the Norman archers and foot-soldiers closed to attack the English, killing and maiming many with their missiles and suffering many casualties in return. The Tapestry glosses this by showing a hail of arrows from William's archers, most of which are being caught on the shields of the English. Shooting uphill, most of their shafts would either have been caught on the shields or passed over the heads of the defenders. The assaults of the archers and the infantry were unable to make any impression on the tightly packed ranks of English, so the cavalry, who had presumably been waiting for openings in the English lines to make their charge, were called into action earlier than would have been usual. The English, says William, were greatly helped by the advantage of the higher ground, which they held in serried ranks without sallying forward, and also by their great numbers and densely packed mass, and moreover by their weapons of war, which easily penetrated shields and other armour. This is presumably an allusion to the much-feared two-handed axes of the housecarls, which were reputedly capable of cutting down horse and rider together at a single blow. Horses are not stupid, and it is extremely difficult to ride them straight at a line bristling with offensive weapons, as Napoleon's cavalry found at Waterloo, when they attempted to charge the unbroken British squares. If, in addition to the axes of the housecarls, the horses had been confronted with English spears positioned as Snorre Sturlason described, William's cavalry would have had quite as difficult a job at Hastings.

It was at this stage, with even the Norman cavalry repelled without any significant advantage gained, that the first note-worthy event of the battle took place. The Bretons in the left wing of the Norman army broke ranks (William of Poitiers says frankly that they turned tail), and retreated, carrying part at least of the central section of the army with them. Indeed, he says, almost the whole of the duke's battle line gave way, a disgrace he excuses by explaining that the Normans believed the duke had been killed. This may have been one of the occasions on which he was unhorsed, rendering him temporarily invisible. The situation was saved only by his presence of mind. Raising his helmet so that his face could be seen, he halted the retreating men and forced them back into the fight again with the flat of his sword, leading the counter-attack against the English right wing that had broken formation to pursue the fleeing enemy.

At this point disagreement over the course of the battle starts. That this first Norman retreat was genuine is not seriously contested by anyone, least of all William of Poitiers who is, as we have seen, refreshingly frank on the subject. What is contentious is the English response. Was the English pursuit the action of ill-disciplined troops who had been instructed to remain within their lines but were unable to resist the impulse to pursue the enemy when they saw them in flight, or was it part of a deliberate counter-attack that went wrong? Harold has been criticized for not launching a full-scale attack at this juncture, with the duke's left wing in disarray and his whole battle line faltering, and if he had done so, he might have been successful. General Fuller thinks that he would have been, that he would easily have annihilated the Norman archers and infantry and that the cavalry would not have drawn rein until they reached Hastings. But the other view holds that his chances of success were no more than 50:50, that, once he left the protection of his strongly defended position, he would have been unable to regain it, and that, on a level plain, his infantry would be very vulnerable to the enemy cavalry, precisely the situation Harold had sought to avoid. He had fought with William in Brittany, he knew the duke would reassert control over his men.

It has been suggested by Lt Colonel C. H. Lemmon that the pursuit of the Bretons by his right wing was part of a planned counter-attack by Harold, and that this would most naturally have been led by his brothers, Earl Gyrth and Earl Leofwine.[c] Their deaths are shown on the Tapestry at just about this stage of the battle; if they had indeed been leading a counter-attack, their fall would certainly have thrown it into disarray, but their deaths might not have been seen by the men on the far right who would have continued to advance as planned, only to find themselves isolated and cut off. On the other hand, the bodies of Gyrth and Leofwine were found close beside their brother at the end of the battle, which is not consistent with them falling at the head of an attack unless there had been an opportunity to retrieve them during a lull in the fighting. It is more likely that the men on the right wing were simply unable to resist the temptation to break ranks and pursue the fleeing Bretons, who were rallied by the duke and rounded on them with the Norman centre, cutting them down. Alfred's army at Wilton had done precisely the same thing, and the Danes had turned on them with equally disastrous results.

At this stage, there seems to have been something of a hiatus in the battle. As Colonel Lemmon points out, troops cannot engage in hand-to-hand fighting for eight hours on end, and both sides would have needed to regroup and rearm. So far, the battle had not gone at all as the duke had expected, since none of his troops, not even the cavalry, had succeeded in making any impact on the English defences; in William of Poitiers' words:

> When the Normans and the troops allied to them saw
> that they could not conquer such a solidly massed enemy
> force without heavy loss, they wheeled round and
> deliberately feigned flight. They remembered how, a
> little while before, their flight had brought about the
> result they desired [i.e., in drawing the English away
> from their defensive position]. . . As before, some
> thousands of them dared to rush, almost as if they were
> winged, in pursuit of those they believed to be fleeing.
> The Normans, suddenly wheeling round their horses,

checked and encircled them, and slaughtered them to
the last man.

Having used this trick twice with the same result,
they attacked the remainder with greater determination:
up to now the enemy line had been bristling with
weapons and most difficult to encircle. So a combat of an
unusual kind began, with one side attacking in different
ways and the other standing firmly as if fixed to the
ground.

Nothing in the story of the battle has provoked more argument
than this question of the feigned flights. Historians have divided
between those who maintain that a feigned flight on the spur of
the moment was much too complicated a manoeuvre for troops
to carry out at that stage of the history of warfare, and those who
point to the occasions on which it had been successfully executed
in the past. Experienced soldiers, like Colonel Lemmon, point
with justice to the problems associated with the manoeuvre, even
in more favourable situations than obtained at Hastings:

A 'feigned retreat' would demand that every man taking
part in it had to know when to retreat, how far to retreat
and when to turn round and fight back; and, moreover,
that these movements had to be carefully synchronized,
or disaster would result. To arrange this in the heat of
battle with men fighting hand-to-hand for their lives
was clearly impossible. Could the operation have been a
carefully rehearsed act, set off, perhaps, by a trumpet
call? Similar acts, performed at military tournaments
and tattoos with the well-drilled and disciplined soldiers
of today need much rehearsal and, even with the small

numbers employed, are difficult enough to stage. Is it possible that a feudal force at the beginning of this millennium could have performed such an act at all? Finally, there is the military maxim, evolved after long years of experience in warfare, that 'troops committed to the attack cannot be made to change direction'. If the situation created by the real flight of some troops was restored by an immediate charge of fresh troops, the result would be much the same as if a 'feigned retreat' had been possible and had taken place, as far as the progress of the battle was concerned. A 'feigned retreat', therefore, the chroniclers made it, in order to save the face of the troops who ran away.[ci]

The Lemmon line is supported by Colonel A. H. Burne in his *Battlefields of Britain,* who writes, 'I simply cannot bring myself to believe that a feigned retreat could have been mounted, as an afterthought, in the midst of the battle', and suggests robustly that the first retreat could be accepted by Norman chroniclers as genuine, since it was the fault of the Bretons, but that the subsequent retreats, which were by Norman troops, had to be presented as something else.

Other historians, however, such as R. Allen Brown, point to the equally convincing reasons for supposing that feigned retreats were possible:

The feigned flight, so the argument runs, cannot have happened because it could not have happened; and it could not have happened because it would have required to a high degree discipline and training which feudal armies, and most especially the exhibitionist knights who formed them, notoriously did not possess. The truth is, of course, that our Frankish knights and Norman knights were as professional as the age could make them, born and bred to war and trained from early youth, in the household which is the contingent of a lord, in the art and science of horsemanship and arms. Not only do we have entirely acceptable, one might almost say overwhelming, evidence for the tactic of the feigned flight employed at Hastings, but we also have further evidence of its practice on other occasions by other knights of this generation – by the Normans at St Aubin-le-Cauf near Arques in 1052–53 and near Messina in 1060, and by Robert le Frison of Flanders at Cassel in 1071. If this is not enough, then we can find much earlier references to the manoeuvre, which was thus evidently a well-known *ruse de guerre,* in e.g. Nithard under the year 842, over two hundred years before Hastings, and in Dudo of St Quentin writing in the first decades of the eleventh century. Clearly of all the arguments which surround the Norman Conquest and Hastings, this one at least must stop.[cii]

It certainly seems perfectly probable that small groups of knights, accustomed from long training to fighting together as a *conroi* or squadron, could have practised and carried out such a manoeuvre, though there would still be the risk of their action being interpreted by the rest of the army (many of whom were foreign mercenaries) as a genuine flight and panic spreading as a result. Bernard S. Bachrach, in his article on the feigned retreats at Hastings,[ciii] shows that the feigned retreat was a common tactic used by the horsemen of the steppes, and points to its use among the Huns, Visigoths and, especially, the Byzantines, who are said by Gregory of Tours to have used it successfully against a body of Franks positioned very much as Harold's forces were at Hastings and with very similar results. Clearly, it must be accepted that feigned retreats were perfectly possible by 1066; with the slight reservation that in this case, all the evidence for them comes to us at second hand, from the winning side, and with the proviso, as pointed out by Colonel Lemmon, that in enemy communiqués, a retreat according to plan was usually interpreted as meaning that the troops had run away.

Whether the retreats were feigned or genuine makes no difference to the outcome. William of Poitiers says that 'some thousands' of the English had rushed out to pursue the retreats and were all killed. Exaggeration of the numbers of the defeated enemy was standard procedure, to make the eventual victory more glorious, just as the English records imply that Harold was seriously outnumbered. It cannot possibly have been as many as 'some thousands' but it was probably enough to cause serious damage to the English defence and to make it necessary for Harold to draw in his wings and shorten his front. This must have made it easier for the Normans to gain access to the ridge and attack him on his flanks, and according to the *Carmen*, they did so. It is irritating that at this point William of Poitiers' chronicle stops reporting the various stages of the battle in favour of a panegyric on the courage and ferocity of the duke. He takes up a more sober account only towards the end of the day when, he says:

> the English army realized that there was no hope of
> resisting the Normans any longer. They knew that they
> had been weakened by the loss of many troops; that the
> king himself and his brothers and not a few of the nobles

of the kingdom had perished; that all who remained were almost at the end of their strength, and that they could hope for no relief.[civ]

In fact there must have been some considerable interval between the two Norman 'feigned' retreats and the collapse that he reports here. William of Poitiers' failure to report the closing stages of the battle in as much detail as the earlier part probably arose from the general fatigue and confusion of those taking part, and their inability to give him the detailed information he needed. We can imagine the growing exhaustion on both sides, the determination of the English to hold their position till after sunset, the desperate efforts of the Normans to assail the English flanks and break through their line to reach the king. Battles lasting as long as Hastings (between eight and nine hours) and indeed Stamford Bridge (probably about seven hours) were extremely rare in the Middle Ages, and it was part of the bad luck of the English that they should have had to fight two of them so close together.

The crucial factor, which William of Poitiers skates over, is the death of Harold. The highly coloured version in the *Carmen*, according to which four knights, one of them the duke himself, burst through the English line and hacked the king down under his standards, is not credible. It is the part reputedly played in this version by the duke that is unbelievable. If it had been true, William of Poitiers would certainly have known of it and equally certainly would have reported it. It would have been a story to rank with the death of Roland at Roncesvalles. It is much more likely that no one on the Norman side knew, in the confusion of the battle, precisely when he was struck, especially if his death or initial disablement was indeed caused by an arrow, and that no one survived on the English side who could have given the facts. There is a tradition, unsupported by surviving evidence, that in the later stages of the battle the duke gave orders to his archers to aim high, so that the arrows dropped on the English from above. This would have overcome the difficulties they would have been caused by the rising ground in their opening volleys, though it would have considerably reduced the penetrative power of the arrows. It would also have enabled the Norman cavalry to charge simultaneously under the archers' cover. If Harold's death was in fact caused by one of the Norman arrows falling from the sky, the arrows were penetrating adequately and William's tactics paid off.

R. Allen Brown, in his account of the battle, said that the only really undisputed fact about Hastings was that the Normans won. One other thing is indisputable, which is that the side whose leader fell first would lose. William had the luck with him throughout his campaign for the throne, but nowhere was that luck more striking than his survival on the battlefield, where he must have been as much if not more at risk as Harold. If he did indeed have three horses killed under him in the course of the battle (and there is no reason to doubt it), then on three occasions at least he was particularly vulnerable not just to the enemy but to being accidentally ridden down by his own knights. It is clear from the first, genuine, flight of the Bretons how quickly the Norman army would have faltered and retreated if he had been killed or incapacitated.

The manner of Harold's death has been almost as much disputed as the retreats, feigned or otherwise. The confusion has been caused partly by the Tapestry, which, in plate 71, shows an armed figure apparently trying to pull an arrow out of his eye and next to him, another armed figure with a battle-axe who is being cut down by a Norman knight. Across the two figures the text reads *Hic Harold Rex interfectus est*, 'Here King Harold is killed'. The word 'Harold' is directly above the figure with the arrow in his eye, the words 'interfectus est' above the figure with the battle-axe. In general, the designer of the Tapestry has taken care to put the name of a character above the person named. The question that has exercised historians is whether both figures depict the dying king or only one of them. Although William of Poitiers could tell us nothing about Harold's death, and little in detail about the later stages of the battle, he does make it clear that the duke had kept up an unceasing barrage of arrows, so the likelihood that the king was struck in the eye by one of them is strong. It is even stronger that, once he was thus disabled, and with his brothers having already fallen, Norman knights would find it easier to burst through the line and hack him down. This section of the tapestry has been subjected to repairs, and efforts have been made to prove, by examining original and newer stitch marks on the reverse, that what now appears to be an arrow in the eye was originally intended to be a javelin that was being thrown by the figure clutching it – not the king but one of his men. It is certainly true that the Tapestry's present state does not necessarily represent the designer's original intention (this is one of the most intensively restored sections), and a very small adjustment of stitches could, quite unintentionally, make a considerable difference to the final effect. Furthermore, blinding was, by Biblical warrant, widely regarded in the Middle Ages as the appropriate punishment for perjury and might therefore be regarded by the Tapestry's designer as particularly appropriate to Harold.

None the less, it is probable that the Tapestry in its original condition showed the king being struck in the eye by an arrow.

Drawings of this part of it made in 1733 before much restoration work had been undertaken show what indubitably looks like an arrow, though it is fair to say that it could also be a javelin, in that no flights are visible on it and the trajectory is pointing a little above the eye. There is also a fairly substantial body of opinion in the century following the battle that the king had been wounded by an arrow. The first to mention it is Amatus of Montecassino (c.1080), who says that Harold was killed by an arrow in the eye. This is corroborated by Baudri de Bourgeuil (c.1100) in the poem he addressed to the duke's daughter, the Countess Adela, in which he describes the hanging in her chamber representing her father's conquest of England. He says that Harold was struck by an arrow, but does not say where. The next version is that of William of Malmesbury (c.1125) who says that the king was wounded by an arrow in the brain and, while lying wounded, was struck on the thigh by a knight with his sword, a very fair description of what is shown in the Tapestry. He was followed by Henry of Huntingdon (c.1130) who tells us that the king was struck in the eye by an arrow and was then killed by wounds. This argues the existence of two different traditions, for neither William nor Henry could have got their version of events from Baudri or Amatus. William's version exactly replicates what seems to be the story in the Tapestry, which possibly pre-dates all of them, though there is no evidence that either William or Henry ever saw it.

We cannot attach much conviction to the contention, frequently maintained, that the designer of the Tapestry would not have shown the king by two separate figures so close together. R. Howard Bloch has drawn attention to the skill of the Tapestry designer in using the techniques of animated cartoons to suggest movement and progression in his portrayal of events; this is most noticeable in, for example, the scene of Harold's embarkation from Bosham at the start of the Tapestry, and in the charge of the Norman knights at the opening of the battle, where a number of figures are depicted in attitudes that, if speeded up, would give the impression of movement.[cv] This depiction of the slaying of Harold may well be another example, showing two images of the same character in progression – though if so, it is noticeable that the king had time to change his stockings in between. Whichever explanation is chosen, it is likely that this scene shows us as much as we are likely ever to know of Harold's death.

It is clear from what William of Poitiers says that part of the English army, probably the housecarls, fought on grimly after the king's death, in the old Germanic tradition, but it is hardly surprising that many of the fyrd melted away into the forest behind them. There is no mention by William of Poitiers of the celebrated Malfosse incident narrated in the *Carmen* and elsewhere, according to which Norman knights, zealously pursuing the retreating English in the dark, rode unawares into a deep ditch on the north of the battlefield and were crushed to death by their companions falling on top of them; since it had no effect on the result of the battle, it can be disregarded, although the exact site of the Malfosse has been a fruitful source of controversy among historians of Hastings. William makes it clear that a considerable number of the English host made a last-ditch stand, supported by what he describes as a 'broken rampart and a labyrinth of ditches' behind the battlefield. For these people, he says, were 'by nature always ready to take up the sword, being descended from the ancient stock of Saxons, the fiercest of men. They would never have been driven back except by irresistible force.'[cvi] But without leadership, there was little they could do except to cause as much damage to the Normans as they could.

They well deserved the tribute of William of Malmesbury: 'they were few in number and brave in the extreme'.

In the meantime, William pitched his tent for the night on the place where Harold's banners had stood, confident that God had judged between him and his enemy. The ruins of Anglo-Saxon England lay scattered around him on the battlefield.

THE AFTERMATH

L ate in his life, Napoleon summed up how wars are won and lost. It was, he said, three parts moral. One part physical.[cvii] Throughout his campaign for the English throne, William had relentlessly maintained the moral high ground, from his manipulation of Harold's oath, through his dealings with the Vatican, to (according to William of Poitiers) his careful arrangement around his neck on the morning of the battle of the bones of the saints on which he maintained Harold had sworn. It has frequently been asserted that in the final analysis he had outgeneralled his opponent, but it was on the moral high ground that he most conspicuously did so. It was a considerable achievement for a man whose conquest lacked any moral or legal justification.

He lost no time in exploiting the propaganda and military victory that he had won, though initially events left him somewhat at a stand. He waited at Hastings, as the D Chronicle records, in the days following the battle for submissions to his authority to come in. They did not come. Instead, as soon as the news of Harold's death reached them in London, the remaining chief men of the kingdom (the two archbishops, Stigand and Ealdred, and Earls Edwin and Morcar among them) elected the young atheling Edgar as king, as clear an indication as could be given of England's rejection of

Norman rule. It was, as even William of Poitiers admitted, evidence of 'their highest wish to have no lord who was not a compatriot'. Perhaps it was only at this stage that William realized exactly how long a struggle lay ahead of him before he could with any realism call the country conquered. The initial stages of the process, the submission of Dover, Canterbury, Winchester, the slaughter of the citizens of Romney who had had the impertinence to attack the Norman ships that had accidentally landed there, the gradual encirclement of London by his army, the devastation of all the territory over which he passed, were soon achieved. London put up more of a fight, but without stronger leadership than a boy of fourteen could provide, it was soon overcome. The unfortunate Edgar, with Stigand and other dignitaries, came to submit to him at Berkhamstead 'out of necessity', says the D Chronicle; and it was great unwisdom that they did not do so earlier, before so much harm was done, it adds bitterly. The Domesday Book gives proof twenty years later of the devastation of the country through which William passed, with large areas of this normally rich and fertile country simply entered as 'waste'. On Christmas Day he was crowned in Westminster Abbey, which thus, in its first year of existence, saw the burial of one king and the coronation of two more.

Again according to William of Poitiers, 'the bishops and other leading men begged him to take the crown, saying that they were accustomed to obey a king, and wished to have a king as their lord'.[cviii] According to the D Chronicle, Archbishop Ealdred refused to place the crown on William's head until he had sworn on the Gospels to be a true lord, and to rule the people as well as any king who had gone before him, provided they would be loyal to him. It is interesting that much the same oath was administered to Cnut on his coronation; it may, in fact, have been standard procedure for all coronations, for English kings as well as for conquerors, but noted only in the case of conquerors. The proviso of English loyalty was to be important to William, since it gave him the only excuse that could be made for the campaign of oppression that followed. Orderic Vitalis claims that, by the grace of God, England was subdued within the space of three months; a somewhat optimistic statement, given that he records later that

> meanwhile the English were groaning under the
> Norman yoke, and suffering oppressions from the proud
> lords who ignored the king's injunctions. The petty lords
> who were guarding the castles oppressed all the native
> inhabitants of high and low degree and heaped shameful
> burdens on them. For Bishop Odo and William
> fitzOsbern, the king's viceregents, were so swollen with
> pride that they would not deign to hear the reasonable
> plea of the English or give them impartial judgement.
> When their men-at-arms were guilty of plunder and
> rape they protected them by force, and wreaked their
> wrath all the more violently upon those who complained
> of the cruel wrongs they suffered.
>
> And so the English groaned aloud for their lost liberty
> and plotted ceaselessly to find some way of shaking off a
> yoke that was so intolerable and unaccustomed.[cix]

There were to be continual risings against the invaders all over the kingdom, but particularly in the north where it looked at one point as if a separate kingdom might be set up under Edgar Atheling, buttressed by his brother-in-law the King of Scotland and King Sweyn Estrithson of Denmark; it was this threat that provoked the infamous harrying of the north by William in

1069–70, a cold-blooded campaign to destroy anything in the area that might support life. Even for chroniclers who normally praised William, this was too much:

> In his anger he commanded that all crops and herds, chattels and food of every kind should be brought together and burned to ashes with consuming fire, so that the whole region north of Humber might be stripped of all means of sustenance. In consequence so serious a scarcity was felt in England, and so terrible a famine fell upon the humble and defenceless populace, that more than 100,000 Christian folk of both sexes, young and old alike, perished of hunger. My narrative has frequently had occasion to praise William but for this act which condemned the innocent and guilty alike to die by slow starvation I cannot commend him. For when I think of helpless children, young men in the prime of life, and hoary greybeards perishing alike of hunger I am so moved to pity that I would rather lament the griefs and sufferings of the wretched people than make a vain attempt to flatter the perpetrator of such infamy.[cx]

Although he may have won the military and propaganda battles, William's victory may in the long term have had some of the flavour of dust and ashes. His initial return to Normandy in triumph with eminent English hostages in his train and wagon-loads of English gold and treasure was hailed with joy, but England was never to be a place where he felt at home and, as the years passed, he spent less and less time there. He had never originally intended to be a conqueror; he had expected a peaceful succession, but his instincts were autocratic. The idea that the

English crown was elective, that the English people could thwart his original intentions, was clearly not one that had ever seriously occurred to him or that he could accept. His initial attempts to learn English were very quickly abandoned; and when the king made no effort to speak the language, it would be hard to blame his underlings for failing to do so. Ironically, even his campaigns in Normandy, Brittany and Maine were much less successful after 1066 than they had been before it. Orderic Vitalis, a reasonably dispassionate critic of the Conqueror, notes that, after 1066,

> because of his remarkable courage he stoutly stood up to all enemies, but he did not invariably enjoy success as before, nor was he cheered by frequent victories. In the thirteen years of life which remained to him he never once drove an army from the field of battle, nor succeeded in storming any fortress which he besieged.[cxi]

What William really wanted from his conquest was the status of a consecrated king, to assist him in his rivalry with the King of France, and the revenues and loot of England. His idea of governing according to the laws of Edward the Confessor (which, in fact, were the laws of Cnut) was to ensure that he received every penny to which he was legally entitled. His conquest was not even to be very durable. Within a century of Hastings, the reign of his own direct Norman line had ended with his daughter's son, King Stephen (the descendants of his own sons having died out), and England and Normandy were settling down under the rule of Angevin kings, descendants of the Geoffrey Martel whom William had fought so desperately earlier in his career.

It is impossible not to contrast his victory with that of Cnut half a century before. Cnut had an advantage linguistically in having a mother-tongue that even at that time was much closer to English than Norman French was (it is notable that in Snorre's account of Stamford Bridge, the Northumbrian English and the Norwegian invaders were able to communicate with each other without much trouble, and a recent study argues convincingly that Old English and Old Norse were mutually intelligible).[cxii] But although his brand of ruthlessness was no less pronounced than William's, he chose, after the bloodbath with which he opened his reign, to operate much more diplomatically, and he made conspicuous efforts to adapt his rule to English custom. The average Englishman would probably have noticed little difference from the rule of his Anglo-Saxon predecessors, apart from the merciful cessation of Viking raids. Cnut did not replace the native ruling class with an alien one; of the three great earls who flourished during his reign and whom he bequeathed to his successors, only one (Siward of Northumbria) was Danish, and he had married into the family of his Northumbrian predecessors. Leofric and Godwin were 'mere English', and this was very much the pattern for the major appointments made throughout his reign. Even if he had wished to, he could not have replaced the senior English churchmen with Danes since Denmark had been too recently converted to Christianity to produce a sufficient number of qualified men. Cnut's rule hardly interrupted Anglo-Saxon rule.

William had rather more excuse for a wholesale importation of a ruling class from abroad, since the three great battles of 1066 had between them virtually wiped out the entire top layer of English society. There is some evidence that he started his reign with the intention of honouring his vow to be a good lord to all his subjects: one of his earliest actions as king was to issue a writ confirming the rights and privileges of the city of London. A number of major landowners were confirmed in their positions (including Earls Edwin and Morcar); Stigand continued in office; and a few English names appear on his earliest charters, though these soon disappear as rebellions surfaced throughout the kingdom. William of Poitiers says that he endowed the boy Atheling with ample lands, but, according to the Domesday Book, Edgar never got possession of any of them. But Edwin and Morcar rebelled in 1068, made their peace with William, then rebelled again in 1071, when they were involved in the rising of Hereward the Wake. Edwin was eventually killed in the fens by his own men, Morcar was captured and spent the rest of his life in prison. We have the testimony of the Domesday Book that by 1086 only 8 per cent of English land remained in the hands of those who had owned it in 1066. William of Malmesbury in the following century confirmed that England had become 'the residence of foreigners and the property of strangers; at the present time there is no Englishman who is either earl, bishop, or abbot; strangers all, they prey upon the riches and vitals of England'.[cxiii]

But there were still possible English appointees left, especially in the Church where a particularly clean sweep of senior English clerics was made; this was no doubt done in part to honour whatever promises may have been made to the Vatican in 1066 (though whatever these were, William maintained Stigand in office as archbishop until 1070). But it certainly caused considerable resentment, since the new Norman bishops and abbots were rarely demonstrably superior to the Englishmen they supplanted and were very often inferior. Edward, Archdeacon of London, who took monastic orders under Lanfranc at Christ Church, Canterbury, is said to have tried to abscond, because he could no longer bear the irritation of being corrected by men less learned than himself. Lanfranc would hardly have come into this category; but then he was a Lombard, not a Norman. The learning and eminence of Lanfranc, previously Abbot of St Stephen's, Caen, and before that prior of Bec, to whose school the students of Europe flocked, was indeed one of the mitigating benefits to England of the conquest. His appointment as Archbishop of Canterbury in 1070 was to be an unqualified advantage to the English Church.

However, there was strong Norman disapproval of the English houses of secular, very often married, canons, set up under the influence of the Lotharingian canonical revival, and a desire to reform them as celibate Benedictine monasteries. The reluctance of some Norman churchmen to accept the old English saints as legitimately canonical was another cause of friction, among both clergy and laity. A certain degree of scepticism was pardonable among the new masters, it was a period in which many things, previously accepted, were being questioned. The great French scholar Abelard even queried the sanctity of France's patron saint, St Denis. But in England, it was also a period in which English sensitivities were very raw. In many monasteries and parishes, the lower clergy, the monks and parish priests, kept their places but in general under foreign superiors. The language gulf between higher and lower increased the English sense of inferiority. English abbeys and churches were pillaged of their treasures, especially if they had had connections with the old regime. King Harold's foundation of secular canons at Waltham Abbey (in which he was probably buried) was stripped of the relics, manuscripts and gold and silver plate with which he had endowed it to enrich William's own foundation of St Stephen's, Caen. Eadmer expresses the general feeling of English churchmen:

Their nationality was their downfall. If they were
English, no virtue was enough for them to be considered
worthy of promotion; if they were foreigners, the mere
appearance of virtue, vouched for by their friends, was
sufficient for them to be judged worthy of the highest
honour.

By 1087, when William died, the only pre-conquest English
bishop still in office was St Wulfstan, Bishop of Worcester.

At what one might call the administrative civil service level,
English officials held on to their posts initially; as long as the
language of government continued to be English, this was
essential, and even after this there is ample evidence in the
Domesday Book that, at the middle levels of society, Englishmen
continued to hold positions, mainly as minor officials, under the
new foreign lords. But as soon as Latin was substituted for English
for official purposes, both in the Church and in government writs,
the way was open for Normans and other foreign clerics to take
their place. William's control over church appointments was rigid,
understandably, since it was his senior churchmen whom he used
most often as regents during his frequent absences from England.

It would be pleasant, though difficult, to believe in the deathbed
speech attributed to him by Orderic Vitalis in which he owned
that he had

wrested [the crown of England] from the perjured King
Harold in a desperate battle, with much effusion of
human blood; and it was by the slaughter and
banishment of his adherents that I subjugated England
to my rule. I have persecuted its native inhabitants
beyond all reason. Whether gentle or simple, I have

cruelly oppressed them; many I unjustly disinherited;
innumerable multitudes, especially in the county of
York, perished through me by famine or the sword. . .
Having, therefore, made my way to the throne of that
kingdom by so many crimes, I dare not leave it to
anyone but God alone, lest after my death worse should
happen by my means.[cxiv]

He then, according to Orderic, handed his second son, William
Rufus, a sealed letter addressed to Lanfranc on his wishes
regarding the appointment of the successor to the throne and
recommended him to cross the sea immediately to secure the
crown for himself. Even in death, it is hard to break the habits of
a lifetime.

It is easy to exaggerate the resentment and humiliation
experienced by the native population as the rule of the conquerors
was established. It is likely that intermarriage between the
conquerors and the conquered began fairly soon after 1066,
possibly in some cases to reinforce title to lands granted to new
masters. There must have been many widows available. To what
extent such marriages were freely entered into cannot now be
known. The official dispensations later granted to Englishwomen
who had entered convents and in some cases taken vows to escape
the predatory attentions of the incomers indicates that such
marriages were not always voluntary. However, to the majority
of a mainly agrarian population (if they did not have the
misfortune to live north of the Humber) life probably continued
much as it had always done, perhaps with rather more emphasis
on the collection of taxes, but subject to the same contingencies of
bad weather, war, harrying and sickness. There was presumably
the added irritation of being ruled by lords who no longer spoke

a language they could understand and who were very often absentee landlords, more concerned with the lands they also held in Normandy or Flanders or with the wars they were fighting on the other side of the Channel, and with the money they could extract from their English estates to pay for them, than with the welfare of their English tenants. It was at the level of the thegns and king's thegns that the new domination would bear hardest. Many of the younger surviving members of these families emigrated, either to Scandinavia or to Constantinople to serve in the Varangian Guard where they would have further chances of fighting the Normans, even if it had to be those of southern Italy.

None the less, what is remarkable is not how much of Anglo-Saxon England was destroyed, but how much in the longer term survived. English laws, language, literature and political and administrative institutions are still recognizably inherited from pre-conquest times. William may have replaced all the chief English office-holders with Normans, Bretons, Flemings and other members of his rather miscellaneous host, but the chief institutions of government he wisely kept intact, since no such efficient and well-regulated arrangements existed at that time in his own duchy. It was these institutions that had made England such a wealthy and desirable country, and since he desired the wealth, he maintained the institutions and to a certain extent, the people who operated them.[cxv] It seems to have been in the cities that the higher classes of the English maintained their standing more than elsewhere. It has been pointed out that, after the conquest, most of the moneyers continued to be English; the family of London moneyers who struck coins for Edward the Confessor and Harold II also struck them for William I, William II and Henry I. Certainly, the standard of the English coinage both before and after 1066 was far higher than that of the Norman coinage and was much more respected internationally. But in general the situation was as summarized by Sir Frank Stenton:

> The Normans who had entered into the English inheritance were a harsh and violent race. They were the closest of all western peoples to the barbarian strain in the continental order. They had produced little in art or learning, and nothing in literature, that could be set beside the work of Englishmen. But politically they were the masters of their world.[cxvi]

It is impossible not to try to guess what would have happened if the battle had gone the other way, as it so easily might. If King Harold had thrown the Normans back into the Channel, he would probably have been secure for the remainder of his reign, as Cnut was. After his death, there would almost certainly have been another disputed succession. He had sons by Edith, who would not have been accepted by the Church as legitimate, and he had at least one much younger posthumous son by Aldyth, sister of Earls Edwin and Morcar, who was legitimate. The former would certainly have put in a claim for themselves, and the claim of the latter would have been supported by his uncles. Depending on when Harold died, there would also have been a strong case for the Atheling Edgar, who would probably have been much of an age with Harold's illegitimate sons, and no older than his great-uncle Edward the Confessor had been when he had succeeded. Harold's election had been prompted by the exceptional dangers threatening England when Edward died, and with those dangers safely surmounted, there would have been nothing against and much to be said for returning to the old royal line. The speed with which the remaining chief men of the kingdom turned to Edgar as soon as Harold's death at Hastings was known indicates that his claim would probably have been strongly supported, especially if the alternative was an internecine contest between members of the Godwinson family. And Edgar, if elected, might perhaps have proved as durable as his great-uncle, as canny a king, and might have done better in the matter of providing an heir. Even as a homeless exile, a wanderer through England, Scotland and France, he outlived almost all the other players in this tragedy.

What would not have happened is easier to guess. The empire constructed by William did not outlast his own life. Normandy was inherited by his rebellious eldest son, Robert; England, which, as he had acquired it by his own efforts he believed (despite his hypothetical deathbed speech) to be his to dispose of at will, went to his second son, William Rufus, and, when William Rufus died childless, to his third son, Henry. Robert's desire to reunite Normandy and England under himself led to a continuous state of war between him and his younger brothers, ending in his loss of Normandy altogether and, eventually, its acquisition by the rival house of Anjou. The fratricidal wars between Robert and his siblings in which England was perforce involved placed the new English aristocracy in a very difficult position. Most of them, certainly the most powerful nobles, held land in both Normandy and England. Those who fought for William Rufus or, after him, Henry risked having their ancestral Norman possessions confiscated by Robert; those who fought for Robert equally risked the loss of their new English lands. Prudent fathers who were able to do so divided their inheritance between two sons, Norman to one, English to the other, thus saving each of them the trouble of choosing sides, though risking the possibility of their later meeting, like the brothers they served, face to face on the battlefield. Many could not or did not do so, and to the curse of being ruled by an alien governing class was added the problem of absentee landlords who expected their English tenants to fight for their masters' lands on the other side of the Channel. The family feuds fought out first between William and his eldest son and, after his death, between all his sons and, indeed, his grandchildren, dragged the English into continuous wasteful and irrelevant warfare, for which in general England paid in lives and money. The situation was not much improved by the accession of Henry II, the first of the Angevin kings and the one who contributed most to the post-conquest development of England, since his continental and family feuds and those of his successors were as incessant as those of his Norman predecessors. England, unconquered, would have been spared all these continental squabbles, although it might have had some succession contests of its own. It is highly unlikely that, on past showing, they would have been as destructive as the civil wars between Stephen and Matilda, after which the direct Norman line died out. More importantly, there would almost certainly have been no Hundred Years War, no English claim to the throne of France, no Agincourt, no burning of Joan of Arc. It might all have been relatively peaceful for England.

It has been suggested that Harold's reign would have turned England politically and culturally more in the direction of Scandinavia, further from the influence of France that was to mean so much to England in the twelfth and thirteenth centuries. This need not have been the case. Harold himself appears to have been a man of some culture, who travelled widely and spoke several languages easily. The English language would almost certainly have developed differently – possibly into something much closer to German or Dutch. Before 1066, English was still heavily inflected; when it re-emerged from obscurity after the conquest, it had lost most of its inflections and agreements. This might have happened spontaneously anyway, though the example of German throws some doubt on the idea. What literature might have been written in it can only be guessed at, but there is no reason to suppose that it would not have been receptive to the new literary fashions on the Continent. Anglo-Saxon England had never been closed to continental influence. Before the conquest, there was (as far as we know) so little vernacular literature elsewhere in Europe that the question hardly arose, but in the other arts there was certainly no isolation. The few artefacts that survive indicate an openness to what was happening elsewhere in Europe that would probably have continued just as easily after 1066 if there had been no invasion – indeed, possibly, much more easily, given the cultural insensitivity of the Norman conquerors in all spheres except architecture. The Carolingian influences in the stole and maniple of St Cuthbert and the work of the extraordinarily beautiful Winchester school of illumination as illustrated in the benedictional of St Æthelwold show to what extent continental examples affected pre-conquest English workmanship.

From the literary point of view, it is less easy to guess what would have happened. It has been suggested that it was the Norman Conquest and the events that followed from it that opened England to the new tide of literary innovation that came from France. This seems unlikely. The Normans were most improbable conduits for any form of culture, and it would be difficult to prove that they were responsible for anything cultural that happened in England in the century that followed 1066; in fact little did, except an outbreak of distinguished historiography, much of it the work of men of dual English and Norman heritage like Orderic Vitalis and William of Malmesbury. A burst of the writing of history frequently follows upheavals such as a conquest; a similar outbreak occurred in Scotland after the Union with England of 1707. It is, perhaps, a way of making sense of the incomprehensible. The tearing apart of the country in the civil wars between Stephen and Matilda left little opportunity for anything in the way of literature or culture to flourish. It was the Angevin court of Henry II and his queen, Eleanor of Aquitaine, that deserves most of the credit for bringing the songs of the troubadours to England and thus for their influence on English lyric poetry, but it is arguable that this would have happened anyway. The absence of anything remotely comparable to the Norman Conquest in Germany and the low countries proved no impediment to the spread of romance and troubadour culture there, any more than in earlier centuries there had been any resistance to the spread of *chansons de geste* on the exploits of Old Germanic heroes like the Volsungs, Attila and the Niblung kings, and Hildebrand and Walther of Aquitaine, in Merovingian or Carolingian France or indeed the rest of western Europe. The twelfth-century lays of Marie de France reached Norway, even Iceland, a country particularly remote from continental influence, without difficulty, certainly without the assistance of any event comparable to the Norman invasion. Poetry, especially oral poetry and song, is notoriously resistant to frontiers.

But perhaps it is appropriate to finish on a vaguely poetic note. We started with the question, how did King Harold contrive to lose a battle that it might rationally have been thought impossible for him to lose. There may be a way of accounting for it, perhaps not in historical or practical terms but in a way that is to some extent artistically and poetically satisfying. To understand it, it is necessary to go back again to the Old Germanic heroic tradition and the concept of heroism, as illustrated in so many of the old legends and, more specifically, in Old English poetry. Heroism, as it is understood in poems like *Beowulf* and *The Battle of Maldon*, is a quality only achieved in death. There is no such thing as a live hero, because there is always the possibility of his fame being tarnished by an unheroic action. Only after death is his heroism fixed and immutable. This is the point of the long speech by Hrothgar to Beowulf, in which he adjures him to avoid the errors of Heremod, an earlier king of the Danes, who in youth performed heroic actions, as Beowulf had done, but later turned to vice and cruelty. It follows that, to attain a heroic reputation, the only kind worth having for a warrior, death in heroic action was to be, if not sought, at least not avoided, even if it was at the expense of prudence or common sense. N. F. Blake makes this point in his essay on the battle of Maldon, and reminds us 'that heroes are not ordinary men. Judged by the standards of rational human behaviour, their gestures are stupid and they provoke comments of apparent criticism', adding that 'rational human behaviour does not provide the appropriate standard to judge by'.[cxvii] It was not sensible for Roland to refuse to blow his horn for help when overwhelmed by superior numbers. It was not sensible for Beowulf, as an old man, to insist on fighting the dragon single-handed; it was certainly not sensible for Byrhtnoth to allow the invading Danes to cross the Blackwater so that they could fight on equal ground. 'God alone knows who shall rule this battlefield,' he says, but one feels he knew. All three were fey: they knew instinctively that the consequences of their actions would be disastrous and that fate had spoken against them, but all knew equally that the challenge with which fate had presented them required them to accept it and die or lose honour and live. The situation faced by Harold was not so very different. From the moment he steps on board the ship that will take him to the swearing of his oath to William, he seems, like them, to move with a dreadful inevitability towards the fate that is waiting for him. It is perhaps fitting that, at the very end of the heroic age, the last Anglo-Saxon King of England should have met his death in a way that his remoter ancestors would have understood and applauded.

THE SOURCES

The existing accounts pose many problems, one of the most important of which is the degree of authority of the sources that have survived, combined with the impossibility of knowing what has been lost, and what light it might have cast on what we now have. The source closest in time to the battle and most generally relied on by historians (William of Poitiers) has survived in a single seventeenth-century text, with material missing at both ends, which was in turn printed from an original, now lost. This gives some idea of the scale of the problem; who knows how corrupt the text may have become between the eleventh and the seventeenth centuries? In addition to the depredations of time there is the silence imposed by political censorship in the period immediately following the conquest. It would not have been prudent for any English chronicler to write down his true feelings about the events of 1066 for many decades after them (although in fact one or two took the risk, as the Waltham Chronicle indicates), nor for any Norman chronicler to write about them other than sycophantically, as most of them did.

None of the surviving sources was written by an eyewitness of the battle. This is not necessarily a disadvantage. Even in periods much nearer our own day, it has generally proved impossible for those taking part in a battle to have more than a very partial, confused impression of what went on. A dispassionate overview could hardly be expected from anyone below the rank of commander-in-chief, and even he could speak only of the actions of his own side. He could only guess at the imperatives that underlay the strategy of his opponent. William of Poitiers (see d. below) excuses himself from mentioning the deeds of all the Normans who took part by making the very fair point that even an eyewitness could hardly have followed everything. This means that all the sources that have survived depend, directly or indirectly, on memory. The memories of two bystanders who witness a road accident are likely to differ, even a very short time after the event; how much more unreliable must be the memories of those who had taken part in so complicated and agonizing an event as a battle lasting many hours.

Some of the sources listed below were written so long after the event that in a different context one might hesitate to trust them at all. In general, testimony as late as that, for example, of William of Malmesbury (see j. below) might not be taken very seriously. But we do not know on what sources William based his account, and that goes for many others of similar date. They might have been good, they might have been bad. In William's case, his version is corroborated in enough cases to make one hesitate to discard his testimony on uncorroborated details too rashly.

With these provisos, let us look at the most important of what has survived more or less in order of date, in so far as any accurate dates can be established.

a. **The Anglo-Saxon Chronicle** The Chronicle, which was reputedly founded by King Alfred towards the end of the ninth century and is written in Old English, was maintained in various monasteries in England, the different surviving versions being distinguished now by letters. The only versions that were still being kept up in 1066 were at Abingdon (C); Worcester (D – this is generally known as the northern version since at that time the episcopal sees of Worcester and York were closely linked but it was more probably written at Worcester); and Peterborough (E), which was probably written at Canterbury, at least during the period with which we are concerned here, and reveals much more detailed information of what was going on in the south of England. It is a feature of the Chronicle generally that different versions tended to include material relevant to the place where they were being maintained that is not found in others, and that each has its own particular bias. E, for example, is notably supportive of the Godwin family; C, by contrast, is anti-Godwinist. Each at various points has irritating silences at points of interest; other sources may tell us that important events happened during these silences, and we can only guess at the reasons why the Chronicle does not notice them. When a version was continued after the conquest, as E was, it may be assumed that some care had to be taken over what was or was not recorded. Thus, it is never safe to assume that, when nothing is recorded in the Chronicle, nothing happened. Examples could be adduced to prove that this was not the case. Of the versions that were being kept up in 1066, E survives only in a twelfth-century copy. C, perhaps surprisingly, does not mention Hastings at all, but ends with the battle of Stamford Bridge, the entry being followed by a short note in a different, later and much less educated hand on the valour of the lone Norwegian who held the bridge while Hardrada's army got itself into fighting order. The entry in the D version has been quoted in the Introduction. E, after a brief description of Stamford Bridge, continues:

> In the meantime Earl William came by sea to Hastings
> on Michaelmass day and Harold came from the north
> and fought with him before all his host had arrived, and
> there he fell, and his two brothers, Gyrth and Leofwine,
> and William overran this land.

We have no way of knowing when the entries in any of the three versions were actually written; it could have been the following month, the following year or several years later. It is possible that the 1066 entry in the D Chronicle was written fairly soon after the year's end since it finishes after the account of William's coronation and return to Normandy with the enigmatic words 'May the end be good when God wills it'.

b. *Carmen de Hastingae Proelio* Attributed (though this has been hotly disputed) to Bishop Guy of Amiens, this is believed to have been written around 1067 (the date too has been disputed) and certainly not later, if the attribution is correct, than Guy's death in 1074 or 1075. This verse narrative is the most controversial source of all. The attribution is based on the twelfth-century statement of Orderic Vitalis (see h. below) that Guy was the author of a poem in the style of Virgil and Statius describing the battle, and on words in the opening of the poem, 'L. W. salutat', which have been interpreted as 'Wido [i.e. Guy] greets Lanfranc' – Lanfranc, Abbot of St Stephen's, Caen, was appointed in 1070 Archbishop of Canterbury. However, this is slender evidence and the claims of the *Carmen* to be a contemporary record have been convincingly challenged by R. H. C. Davis[cxviii] who places its date about the middle or second half of the twelfth century. One of his most persuasive arguments is that details in the *Carmen* not also found in the chronicle of William of Poitiers (see d. below) to which it has marked similarities, such as the legend of Taillefer, are usually found only in later sources such as Henry of Huntingdon and Wace. Another is the sheer incredibility of this version of the death of Harold at the hands of four knights, led by Duke William, which certainly bears all the hallmarks of embroidery on the original story well after the time when all the alleged participants were dead. The elements of the *Carmen* that seem more credible could all have been derived from earlier accounts such as William of Poitiers'. Davis's arguments, however, have been equally convincingly disputed by E. M. C. van Houts,[cxix] who supports the early date of the poem and its association with the bishop. To some extent, the jury is still out on this one. There may, as Orderic Vitalis says, have been a poem on the battle by Bishop Guy of Amiens, and this may be it, but there is some doubt. Since there is a reasonable case for accepting that it is by the bishop, it has been retained in the list of sources, though without accepting its reliability on any uncorroborated points of importance. Guy of Amiens was not a Norman, and one might therefore expect to look to him for a more impartial account of events than might have come from a Norman chronicler; but the bishop was a native of Ponthieu, a county that had been under Norman rule for some years by 1066; his nephew Guy was the Count of Ponthieu who captured Harold on his shipwreck and handed him over to William. His younger nephew, Hugh of Ponthieu, brother of Guy, took part in the battle where his deeds and gallantry lose nothing in his uncle's account. Hugh was certainly not the only participant in the action whom the bishop would have known, so there is no doubt that he would have had eyewitness accounts to draw on. Assuming that he is indeed the author, the questions are to what extent he felt himself bound by strict accuracy in a poem clearly intended for entertainment, in which he might well have felt that

he had a greater degree of artistic licence than in a sober prose
chronicle, and how far we can distinguish fact from fiction in his
work. He starts his narration at St. Valéry to which William had
moved his fleet before the invasion, and where he was weather-
bound by contrary winds. He follows him across the Channel,
reports the exchange of embassies with the king and then gives a
fairly detailed description of the battle, in which he describes many
natural features of the field very much as they are known to have
been (he speaks, for example, of a hill and a valley on Harold's
side of the field, and of land too rough to be tilled), though his
sequence of events is rather confused. He reports, additionally,
the fact that the English stood in such dense formation that the
dead could not fall, and he also reports the retreats, feigned or
real, of the Normans that lured some of the English out of their
defensive lines. Finally, he tells of the four knights, Duke William,
Guy's nephew Hugh of Ponthieu, Eustace of Boulogne (brother-
in-law of King Edward and another kinsman of the author) and
a knight called Giffard (or Gilfard), who cut King Harold down
at the foot of his standard. It is this report, above all, that discredits
the poem as a reliable account of the battle. Against the
improbability of this version of the king's death must be set the
fact that, if Guy were the author, he knew at least three of these
knights well; all survived the battle, and would thus have had the
opportunity of hearing and if necessary, challenging his version
of their deeds. The account then follows William to London and
to his coronation on Christmas Day. What he does not cover is
any of the period preceding Harold's accession, though he refers
in passing to Harold's oath to William. He eulogizes William
throughout, comparing him to Caesar in the opening lines. His
description of the ravaging of the country around Hastings after
William's landing demonstrates his general attitude and tone:

Guarding the shore and fearing to lose your ships, you
protect them with ramparts and pitch camp there. You
repair the remnants of earlier fortifications and set
guards to protect them. With peace, indeed, but little
ground acquired, your men go out and devastate and
burn the land – behaviour which, since the stupid people
reject you as king, is not to be wondered at. It is entirely
just that they should perish and come to naught.

c. **Gesta Normannorum Ducum** William of Jumièges' chronicle
ends in 1069, from which it has been assumed that it would have
been completed by about 1071. It appears to have been a popular
work, for many manuscripts of it have survived. It is a history of
the Dukes of Normandy mainly based on an earlier work, but
with a final section on the conquest; it is dedicated to the duke
and, as might be expected, is openly partisan. The author narrates
the story of Edward the Confessor's undertaking that William
should be his successor, the story of Harold's oath and the breaking
of it, and the appearance of Halley's comet. He describes the
assembly of William's army and fleet (3,000 vessels), the crossing
to Pevensey, the battle and its aftermath, and the duke's coronation
in London. His account has been somewhat discredited by his
apparent statement that Harold fell in the first attack, which
would be difficult to believe, since it would make nonsense of the
generally accepted version that the English only broke, late in the
day, on hearing of his death; but this peculiarity is generally
accepted to be the result of error in an early translation of the text.

d. **Gesta Guillelmi Ducis Normannorum** William of Poitiers
wrote this chronicle from 1073 to 1074. His military experience
gives some added authority to his references to military matters,

but he is shamelessly sycophantic of the duke. Unlike the work of William of Jumièges, of which there are many manuscripts, only one version (and that incomplete) has survived, beginning with the death of Cnut in 1035 and ending in 1067; but what is assumed to be part at least of the missing section is supplied by Orderic Vitalis (see h. below) who based his own *Historia Ecclesiastica* on it and tells us that it originally ended in 1071. Other evidence shows many of William's statements to be slanted or simply wrong, causing the reader to regard with some suspicion those on which we have, unfortunately, no cross-check, such as Duke William's dealings with the Pope in 1066. His knowledge of classical literature enabled him to move easily among the works of Virgil, Lucan, Sallust and Caesar, selecting the historical episodes with which William's exploits could advantageously be compared, but also arousing the suspicion that certain of these could have been manufactured or adjusted to allow such comparisons to be cited. There are clear points of correspondence between his work and the *Carmen;* one of them has undoubtedly borrowed from the other, unless both used the same sources, oral or written, now lost. The tone throughout has been described by a partisan of the Norman side as displaying 'the arrogance of success and the brutality of triumph'.

e. **Vita Ædwardi Regis** This is a biography of King Edward the Confessor by an anonymous cleric, possibly Flemish or Lotharingian and possibly a monk of St Omer (he refers to the English as 'that race' but shows little sympathy for Edward's Norman friends), written at the instance of his queen Edith, daughter of Earl Godwin, to celebrate the achievements of the house of Godwin. This stops short at the king's death, before Harold's short reign and the invasion itself, though a degree of foreknowledge of future events indicates that it was concluded after the conquest. It is primarily of interest here for information about the Godwin family, in particular the characters of two of the main players, Harold and Tostig, whom the writer probably knew and whom he describes with some shrewdness. It must be assumed that for much of the content he was dependent on Edith, who commissioned it, which may explain its decidedly pro-Tostig stance as he appears from it to have been her favourite brother. Its date is uncertain; it was probably finished before Edith's death (1075), but what is not certain is whether the first and most interesting part was written before the battle, the outcome of which is hinted at but not actually mentioned. It may all be post-1066. The manuscript itself has been dated c.1100.

f. **Historia Novorum in Anglia** Written between c.1095 and 1123 by Eadmer, a monk in the abbey of Christ Church, Canterbury, most of this history concerns later events than Hastings. Eadmer does not describe the actual battle, but the short account of Harold's visit to Normandy and the subsequent conquest is illuminating, especially when compared with the account of, for example, William of Poitiers. Like almost all the English chroniclers, he sees the English defeat as God's retribution for Harold's broken oath. His version is the nearest we can get to an English perspective after the Anglo-Saxon Chronicle; but Christ Church was a notably pro-Godwinist establishment. On the other hand, it is possible that, in Bishop Æthelric, who had been a monk of Christ Church and whom he certainly consulted over his life of St Dunstan, he had access to the memories of a kinsman of Earl Godwin and may therefore have had information about his sons not known to other writers (see p. 53 above).

g. *The Chronicle of Florence of Worcester* (sometimes known as the Chronicle of John of Worcester) This forms part of a continuation of the world chronicle of Marianus Scotus (d. 1082) but its most valuable part is the section on English history from 450 to 1140. Based largely on a version of the Anglo-Saxon Chronicle, now lost, he adds information that supplements surviving versions that, especially when it concerns events of relevance to Worcester, cannot be easily disregarded, although his work, which must have been concluded after 1140, was written later than other sources. It is, for example, on his authority that it is accepted that Harold was crowned by Archbishop Ealdred of York; since Ealdred had formerly been Bishop of Worcester, and was succeeded there by Bishop Wulfstan under whom John worked (and who was almost certainly present at the ceremony), this is better authority than any of the Norman sources, which assert that the ceremony was performed by Archbishop Stigand of Canterbury, then under papal interdict.

h. *Historia Ecclesiastica* Orderic Vitalis (c.1123–24), a monk of half-English, half-Norman parentage, did not write until the twelfth century, like Florence of Worcester. A Benedictine monk born in Shrewsbury of an English mother and a Norman father, he was sent by the latter in 1085 to the monastery of St Evroult in Normandy, where he seems to have spent the rest of his life. His work was intended, like Bede's, to be concerned with church affairs; his description of the Norman Conquest (in book 3) is a distraction from this objective. His aim, he said, was to tell the simple truth, impartial between English and Normans, and he does go some way to correct the bias of William of Jumièges and William of Poitiers on whose work he relied.

i. **Roman de Rou** Maistre Wace wrote about a century after the event (c.1160–70), in Norman French, and has therefore generally been dismissed as unreliable, but he spent much of his life in the neighbourhood of Caen in the company of those who could give him first-hand accounts; his estimate of the number of ships (696) taken by William to England, for example, given to him, as he tells us, by his father, is now regarded as more likely to be accurate than the more inflated figures in some of the earlier accounts, for example William of Jumièges; on the other hand, he is clearly writing for entertainment rather than as a sober historian, and it is unwise to accept his version of events unless they can be corroborated elsewhere. He is less likely to be reliable on purely English events for which he must have been dependent on hearsay and legend. He includes the story of Harold's brother, Gyrth, attempting to persuade Harold to let him lead the English forces, since he had sworn no oath, and also the story that the envoy sent by William to Harold before the battle threatened the English with excommunication. In his version of Harold's visit to Normandy, however, he gives the versions of William of Jumièges and William of Poitiers, but also the version of Eadmer, and says frankly that he does not know which is truthful. He may well be correct in many of his statements, possibly he often is; but we have no check.

j. **Gesta Regum** William of Malmesbury composed his chronicle about 1125 apparently at the request of Henry I's queen (the great-granddaughter of King Edmund Ironside and the last survivor of the old royal family of Wessex). William had at least some of the instincts of a true historian; he compares his sources and points out contradictions in the evidence. But we have no means of knowing in many cases how authoritative some of his sources were. Though he is thought to have had some English blood, he writes avowedly as a Norman ('to whom [i.e. Normans] I am strongly bound, both by my descent and for the advantages I enjoy') and, though he regards Harold as a usurper, as his Norman loyalties oblige him to do, he is very divided in his account of him, telling us that Harold would have governed the kingdom with prudence and with courage, had he come by it lawfully. He is also the main source of the story that Harold did not share out the booty from Stamford Bridge before marching south, which caused many men to desert from him. This occurs also in Geffrei Gaimar's *L'Estoire des Engleis* (1136–37), who may have taken it from William of Malmesbury or (since the two books were written very close together in terms of dates) may have had a different source; but Gaimar's tendency to the creative embroidery of his material inspires little confidence in him as an independent witness.

k. ***King Harald's Saga in Heimskringla*** Snorre Sturlason's saga includes an account of the battle of Stamford Bridge that immediately preceded Hastings. Snorre was writing two centuries after the event, relying on the songs and legends of the court poets who were his predecessors, and has been generally dismissed as an unreliable source; but it has been pointed out that the most striking inaccuracies in his account (for example, English names and family relationships) are things of which an Icelandic writer might reasonably be ignorant, while his account of the battle of Stamford Bridge and the English tactics at it (other than the English use of cavalry in the battle) have in some details been corroborated elsewhere. The chief problem with his account is that, by the time he wrote, in the thirteenth century, the legends that had attached themselves to both Stamford Bridge and

Hastings a fortnight later had become intertwined and confused and it is difficult now to untangle them. The one point that should be remembered is that the Norwegian versions of the battle, on which Snorre built his saga, derive from the memories and stories of the Norwegian survivors who took Hardrada's body back with them, and therefore have a validity independent of the later English sources.

l. **Bayeux Tapestry** This is the most extraordinary source of all: a piece of embroidery that provides a cartoon history of the Norman Conquest from roughly 1054 to the closing hours of the battle (the final panels are missing but probably originally concluded with William's coronation). For many years this was thought to have been commissioned by Odo, Bishop of Bayeux and half-brother of William, and this is generally accepted although it has been suggested that Count Eustace of Boulogne (who is certainly shown as playing a disproportionately large part in the battle) may have been responsible for it. It seems to have been designed to tell the story from the Norman perspective and it mainly corroborates the versions given by William of Jumièges and William of Poitiers. But it is almost certainly of English workmanship and was probably executed at Canterbury, a noted centre of English embroidery and a place with which Odo, as Earl of Kent, had close connections; and in some ways the subtext of the story it tells is strangely ambivalent, as has been seen. It is noticeable, for example, that though William's very spurious claim to the English crown depended on his inheriting it directly and immediately from Edward the Confessor, so that it was essential to it that Harold should always be portrayed as a usurper, Harold is always described in the Tapestry after the death of Edward as 'Harold Rex' and is, on the whole, shown sympathetically and with dignity.

In the Domesday Book, on the contrary, he is referred to exclusively (apart from one or two oversights) as 'Earl Harold'. It is interesting that he makes more appearances in the Tapestry than William: the story it tells is, in a very real sense, the Aristotelian tragedy of Harold, of the great man brought down by a fatal flaw. We know that the Tapestry was exhibited annually in the cathedral of Bayeux to celebrate the Feast of the Relics, assumed to be the relics on which Harold swore; this accounts for the scene of the oath being shown on the Tapestry as Bayeux, although William of Poitiers places it at Bonneville. Thus the Tapestry may be read as a religious lesson to the illiterate faithful on the fatal consequences of perjury. It may also be seen as the work of a designer who did not see the issue in quite such black and white terms as his patron.

It is vital to emphasize that we actually do not know precisely when the Tapestry was worked; a good case has been made for its origin in the years before the fall and disgrace of Bishop Odo in 1082. This is important, if only because of the tendency of historians and other writers (among whom I include myself) to use details in the Tapestry as evidence for and confirmation of details in written sources, when in fact, if it were of a later date, it might have been influenced by them. If, as a purely hypothetical example, the Tapestry had been the work of the embroiderer of the hanging depicting the battle that, according to Baudri de Bourgeuil (see below), hung in the chamber of Duke William's daughter, or if both had been influenced by a common source, now lost, it would hardly be surprising that it appears to show Harold being killed by an arrow, since Baudri is one of the few sources to give this detail; if it had a totally independent origin, both it and Baudri would have much more credibility and would reinforce each other's evidence. But, as with so much else, we don't know when it was worked or by whom; we can only guess.

There are other sources that mention the battle, mostly only incidentally, but that give details not provided elsewhere. The Latin poem of Baudri, Abbot of Bourgeuil, *Adelae Comitissae* (c.1100), addressed to William's daughter, speaks of a hanging in her chamber depicting her father's victory over the English and asserts that Harold was killed by an arrow; his account is corroborated in a history of the Normans (c.1080) by Amatus of Montecassino, who says that Harold was hit in the eye by an arrow. On the other hand, it has been suggested that Baudri's hanging is an imaginary re-creation of the Bayeux Tapestry, which he might have seen at Bayeux or elsewhere; if this were true, his corroboration of the king being struck by an arrow would be valueless. There are also the later accounts of Henry of Huntingdon (*Historia Anglorum,* c.1123–33) in which the battle is covered fairly briefly, and the *Chronicle of Battle Abbey* (probably late twelfth century), both of which preserve fragments of information that may be authentic among much that is almost certainly not. The Battle Abbey chronicler, for example, is the only source to give the information that the Normans first spotted the English army emerging from the woods when they paused at Hedgland on Telham Hill to arm themselves. This is exactly the kind of local tradition about a local holding that is likely to have been remembered locally and to have been unknown to other chroniclers. On other matters, the Battle Abbey account is of little use. There are, too, the annals of Nieder-Altaich, which mention that in 1066 the Aquitainians fought and defeated the English in a naval battle; whether this is a confused version of Hastings itself, or corroboration of the statement in the E text of the Anglo-Saxon

Chronicle that Harold launched a sea attack on William in 1066 shortly before Tostig's raid on England cannot now be established.

There is one further factor that should be taken into account in the consideration of these sources. All of them, with the exception of Henry of Huntingdon (a cleric but not a monk) and Snorre Sturlason and just possibly the Bayeux Tapestry, are monastic productions. This has important implications. This was the age of the trial by ordeal, and the justice of a cause was proclaimed by the outcome of the trial. All these authors would have believed devoutly in the divine justice, manifested by the outcome of the trial. English misfortunes and defeats are commonly recorded throughout the Anglo-Saxon Chronicle, from Alfred's wars against the Danes onwards, with the formula 'as God granted it for the sins of the people'. Harold is reported by many of these historians to have exclaimed the night before the battle that God would judge between William and him. To those who wrote about the event afterwards, on both sides, it would appear clear that He had done so.

NOTES

i   *The Hot Gates*, Faber 1970, p.20.

ii   The ealdorman, a nobleman who was very often a member of the royal family, was appointed by the king (it was not a hereditary title) and was responsible for the welfare and good government of his shire, for maintaining the king's rights in it and organizing its defence.

iii   The title 'Atheling' generally signified a prince born of the royal blood and eligible, in principle, to become king. It was normally given only to the son of a reigning king.

iv   Handfast marriage was marriage without the benefit of clergy; the term derived from the Old Norse term, *handfesta,* to strike a bargain by the joining of hands and such marriages were common in England and elsewhere and generally known as marriage *more Danico*, although the Danes do not seem to have been any more addicted to it than many other nations. The great advantage of it was that it did not prohibit a political or diplomatic marriage at a later date. Cnut's liaison with Ælfgifu of Northampton was probably such an arrangement, since he was clearly regarded as free to marry Emma during Ælfgifu's lifetime.

v   Sir Frank Stenton, *Anglo-Saxon England*, Oxford 1962, pp.401–02 (cited in future as 'Stenton').

vi   *Encomium Emmae,* ed. Alistair Campbell, Cambridge University Press 1998, pp.41–42. It has been suggested (Pauline Stafford, *Queen Emma and Queen Edith*, Blackwell 1997, p.245) that both

Edward and Alfred came, but separately, and that Edward beat a hasty retreat on finding less support than he had expected.

vii   Frank Barlow, *Edward the Confessor,* 1979, p.72.

viii   Ælfric, *Catholic Homilies*, (cited in future as Barlow) ed. B. Thorpe, Ælfric Society, London 1844, I, p. 212.

ix   William of Poitiers, *Gesta Guillelmi,* (quoted in future as *GG),* ed. and trans. R. H. C. Davis and Marjorie Chibnall, Oxford Medieval Texts, Clarendon Press 1998, p.19.

x   David C. Douglas, 'Edward the Confessor, Duke William of Normandy, and the English Succession', *English Historical Review* (1953), pp.526 ff.

xi   Eric John, 'Edward the Confessor and the Norman Succession', *English Historical Review,* 371 (1979), pp.255–56.

xii   David C. Douglas, *William the Conqueror*, University of California Press 1964, pp.59–60.

xiii   *The Waltham Chronicle*, ed. and trans. Leslie Watkiss and Marjorie Chibnall, Oxford Medieval Texts, Clarendon Press 1994, p.45.

xiv   Eric John, *op. cit.,* p.260.

xv   R. Allen Brown, *The Normans and the Norman Conquest*, Boydell Press 2000, p.114.

xvi   *The Life of King Edward who Rests at Westminster*, ed. and trans. Frank Barlow, Clarendon Press, Oxford 1992 (cited in future as *Vita Ædwardi Regis*) p.51.

xvii   Richard Gameson points out that this is one of the four times when the bare Tapestry narrative includes any descriptive or adjectival comment, which gives the phrase added significance ('The Origin, Art and Message of the Bayeux Tapestry', *The Study of the Bayeux Tapestry*, ed. R. Gameson, Boydell and Brewer, Woodbridge 1997, p.187).

xviii   Eadmer, *History of Recent Events in England*, trans. Geoffrey Bosanquet, The Cresset Press 1964, p.6.

xix   *Ibid.*, p.8.

xx   Ian W. Walker, *Harold, the Last Anglo-Saxon King*, Sutton Publishing, Stroud 2004, pp.228–30.

xxi   James Campbell, 'Norwich' in M. D. Lobel (ed.), *The Atlas of Historic Towns*, 1975, II, 1.

xxii   Patrick Wormald, *The Making of English Law: King Alfred to the Twelfth Century*, Blackwell, Oxford 2001 (cited in future as Wormald), p.x

xxiii   James Campbell, *The Anglo-Saxons*, Penguin Books, London 1991, pp.244–45.

xxiv   R. W. Chambers, *England Before the Norman Conquest*, Longman Green & Co. 1926, pp.229–30.

xxv   Stenton, p.473.

xxvi   *GG,* p.153.

xxvii   *The Beginnings of English Society*, Penguin 1982, p.61. I am much indebted to Professor Whitelock's invaluable book throughout this chapter.

xxviii   There is no similar record of gifts sent to Athelstan four years later when Henry the Fowler, King of Germany, asked for an English bride for his son Otto. Athelstan sent two more of his half-sisters, Eadgyth and Ælfgifu, presumably so that the king could have a choice. Eadgyth was chosen; Ælfgifu was later married to Konrad the Peaceable of Burgundy.

xxix   *Historia Anglorum*, ed. T. Arnold, London 1879, pp.5–6.

xxx   *Ælfric's Colloquy*, ed. G. A. Garmonsway, Methuen's Old English Library 1961, pp.33–34.

xxxi   C. R. Dodwell, *Anglo-Saxon Art*, Manchester University Press 1982, p.219.

xxxii   Dorothy Whitelock, *op. cit.,* pp.223–24.

xxxiii   Manchester University Press, 1982.

xxxiv   *Encomium Emmae Regina,* ed. Alistair Campbell, Cambridge University Press 1998, pp.19–21.

xxxv   Dodwell, *op. cit.*, p.30.

xxxvi   Dodwell, *op. cit.*, pp.33–34.

xxxvii   Dodwell, *op. cit.*, p.35.

xxxviii The precise nature of her relationship has never been clear but was obviously long-standing since it produced several children. It cannot have been blessed by the Church, since Harold was able to make a political marriage to the daughter of Earl Ælfgar in 1066, while Edith was, it is assumed, still alive.

xxxix   *Domesday Book: a complete translation*, ed. Ann Williams and G. H. Martin, Penguin 2003, p.856.

xl   *Ibid.*, p.410.

xli   *op. cit.*, p.191.

xlii   *Asser's Life of King Alfred*, Penguin 1988, p.90.

xliii   James Campbell, *Essays in Anglo-Saxon History*, Hambleden
        Press 1986, p.158.

xliv   Frank Barlow, *The English Church* 1000–1066, Longman 1963,
        p.38.

xlv   David Bates, *William the Conqueror*, Tempus 1989, p.159.

xlvi   *Ecclesiastical History*, vol. II (quoted in future as *Eccl. Hist.*), ed.
        and trans. Marjorie Chibnall, Oxford Medieval Texts, Oxford
        1990, p.39. In fairness he adds that the charter was also
        witnessed with a cross by William's uncle Mauger, Archbishop
        of Rouen, who (one would hope) could have written his name.
        On the other hand he records, as a matter of surprise, that
        William's son Henry 'acquired some literacy' when he reached
        the age for schooling (*Ibid.*, p.215) and thus presumably the
        soubriquet *Beauclerc*. The implication that Henry's brothers
        failed to do so is inescapable.

xlvii   David Bates, *Normandy Before* 1066, Longman 1982, p.xiii.

xlviii trans. R. K. Gordon, *Anglo-Saxon Poetry*, J. M. Dent 1962,
        pp.100–101.

xlix   trans. R. K. Gordon, *Anglo-Saxon Poetry*, J. M. Dent 1962, p.300.

l   *Ibid.*, p.236.

li   W. P. Ker, *The Dark Ages*, Nelson 1955, p.57.

lii   Vegetius, *De Re Militari*, 69.

liii   Richard Abels, *Alfred the Great*, Pearson Education 1998,
        pp.198–99.

liv   *Domesday Book*, p.136.

lv   C. Warren Hollister, *Anglo-Saxon Military Institutions on the Eve
        of the Norman Conquest*, Clarendon Press 1962, p.84.

lvi   *English Historical Documents* 1042–1189 (quoted in future as
        EHD), ed. David C. Douglas and George W. Greenaway,
        London 1981, p.905.

lvii   *GG*, p.107.

lviii   *English Historical Review*, XXV (1910), 287–93.

lix   R. Allen Brown, *The Normans and the Norman Conquest*, The
        Boydell Press 2000, p.39.

lx   'Military Service in Normandy before 1066', *Anglo-Norman
          Warfare,* ed. Matthew Strickland, The Boydell Press 1992, p.29.
lxi   B. S. Bachrach, 'Some observations on the military
          administration of the Norman Conquest', *Proceedings of the
          Battle Conference on Anglo-Norman Studies,* viii.
lxii   *GG*, p.103.
lxiii   There are many more specialized publications available on the
          subject.
lxiv   Snorre Sturlason, *King Harald's Saga,* trans. Magnus Magnusson
          and Hermann Pálsson, Penguin 1966, p.151.
lxv   *Ibid.*, p.148.
lxvi   Wormald, p.133.
lxvii   Barlow, p.240.
lxviii   Barlow, p.246.
lxix   *EHD*, p.225.
lxx   Ann Williams, *Kingship and Government in Pre-Conquest
          England, c.*500–1066, Macmillan 1999, p.148.
lxxi   *EHD,* pp.225–26.
lxxii   *GG,* p.103.
lxxiii   David C. Douglas, *William the Conqueror,* University of
          California Press 1964, p.184.
lxxiv   H. A. L. Fisher, *History of Europe,* Edward Arnold, London
          1936, p.199.
lxxv   He was granted the pallium by Pope Benedict X, himself
          deposed as an 'intrusive' pope almost immediately afterwards,
          which compounded his illegality.
lxxvi   *EHD*, p. 691.
lxxvii   John Julius Norwich, *The Middle Sea,* Vintage 2007, p.119.
lxxviii   Catherine Morton, 'Pope Alexander II and the Norman
          Conquest', *Latomus,* XXXIV, 1975, pp.362–82.
lxxix   Walker, *op. cit.*, p.169.
lxxx   *The Chronicle of Battle Abbey,* ed. and trans. Eleanor Searle,
          Oxford Medieval Texts, Oxford 1980, pp.20–21.
lxxxi   *EHD*, p.226.
lxxxii   *Domesday Book,* p.979.
lxxxiii   *GG*, p.109.
lxxxiv   R. Allen Brown, *op. cit.*, p.135.

lxxxv   Snorre Sturlason, *King Harald's Saga*, trans. Magnus Magnusson and Hermann Pálsson, Penguin 1966, p.147.

lxxxvi   *Ibid.*

lxxxvii   *Ibid.*, pp.149–50.

lxxxviii   *Ibid.*, p.152.

lxxxix   Guy of Amiens, *Carmen de Hastingae Proelio*, ed. and trans. Frank Barlow, Clarendon Press 1999, p.5. Quoted in future as *Carmen*.

xc   'The Pevensey Campaign: brilliantly executed plan or near disaster?' in *The Battle of Hastings,* ed. Stephen Morillo, Boydell and Brewer 1999, p.139.

xci   *GG*, p.117.

xcii   *GG*, pp.121–23.

xciii   *Vita Ædwardi Regis,* p.53.

xciv   John Gillingham, 'William the Bastard at War', *Anglo-Norman Warfare*, ed. Matthew Strickland, Boydell Press 1992, p.158.

xcv   *EHD*, p.227.

xcvi   *The Waltham Chronicle*, p.49.

xcvii   J. F. C. Fuller, 'The Battle of Hastings 1066' in *The Battle of Hastings*, ed. Stephen Morillo, Boydell and Brewer 1999, p.167.

xcviii   It is highly unlikely that cross-bows were used at Hastings and none is illustrated in the Bayeux Tapestry. The word 'balistus' used by William of Poitiers may mean a sling for stones.

xcix   *GG*, p.127.

c   Whitelock, Douglas, Lemmon and Barlow, *The Norman Conquest, its setting and impact*, Eyre and Spottiswoode 1966, pp.107–08.

ci   *Ibid.*, pp.109–10.

cii   R. Allen Brown, 'The Battle of Hastings' in *The Battle of Hastings*, ed. Stephen Morillo, Boydell and Brewer 1999, pp.212–13.

ciii   Bernard S. Bachrach, 'The Feigned Retreat at Hastings', in *The Battle of Hastings*, ed. Stephen Morillo, Boydell and Brewer 1999.

civ   *GG*, p.137.

cv   R. Howard Bloch, *A Needle in the Right Hand of God,* Random House 2006, pp.167–69.

cvi   *GG,* p.139.

cvii   *Correspondance de Napoléon 1er* (1858–69), vol. 15.

cviii   *GG,* p.149.

cix   Orderic Vitalis, *Ecclesiastical History*, ed. and trans. Marjorie
         Chibnall, Oxford Medieval Texts 2002, bk. IV, p.203.

cx   *Ibid.,* p.233.

cxi   *Ibid.*, p.351. William did not die until 1087.

cxii   M. Townend, *Language and History in Viking Age England:
         Linguistic Relationships between Speakers of Old Norse and Old
         English*, Turnhout, 2002.

cxiii   William of Malmesbury, *History of the Kings of England*, II,
         §227.

cxiv   *EHD*, p.311.

cxv   A detailed account of the survival of Englishmen under the
         Normans can be found in Ann Williams, *The English and the
         Norman Conquest*, Boydell and Brewer 2000.

cxvi   *Anglo-Saxon England,* Oxford 1962, p.678.

cxvii   N. F. Blake, 'The genesis of *The Battle of Maldon*', *Anglo-Saxon
         England* 7 ed. Peter Clemoes, Cambridge University Press 1978,
         p.124.

cxviii   R. H. C. Davis, 'The *Carmen de Hastingae Proelio*', *EHR*, vol.
         93, no. 367 (April 1978), pp.241–61.

cxix   'Latin Poetry and the Anglo-Norman Court 1066–1135: *The
         Carmen de Hastingae Proelio*', *Journal of Medieval History* 15
         (1989), pp.39–62.

BIBLIOGRAPHY

Primary texts

Anglo-Saxon Chronicle: *Two of the Saxon Chronicles parallel*, ed. Earle and
   Plummer, OUP 1952, 2 vols.
Ælfric, *Colloquy*, ed. G. A. Garmonsway, Methuen's Old English Library,
   1961.
Anglo-Saxon Poetic Records, 6 vols., George Routledge & Sons, 1931–53.
Asser, *Life of King Alfred*, ed. and trans. Simon Keynes and Michael
   Lapidge, Penguin, London 1983.
The Chronicle of Battle Abbey, ed. and trans. Eleanor Searle, Oxford
   Medieval Texts, Oxford University Press 1980.
Bede, *A History of the English Church and People*, trans. Leo Sherley-Price,
   Penguin, London 1955.
Beowulf and The Fight at Finnesburg, ed. Fr. Klaeber, D. C. Heath & Co.,
   1950.
R. W. Chambers, *England Before the Norman Conquest*, Longmans,
   London 1926.
Domesday Book: a complete translation, ed. Ann Williams and G. H.
   Martin, Penguin, London 2003.
Eadmer, *History of Recent Events in England*, trans. Geoffrey Bosanquet,
   The Cresset Press 1964.
Encomium Emmae Reginae, ed. Alistair Campbell, Cambridge University
   Press 1998.
English Historical Documents:.
   500–1042, ed. Dorothy Whitelock, Eyre Methuen, London 1955.

1042–1189, ed. David C. Douglas and George W. Greenaway, Eyre Methuen, London 1981.

The Life of King Edward who rests at Westminster, ed. and trans. Frank Barlow, Clarendon Press, Oxford 1992.

Guy of Amiens, *Carmen de Hastingae Proelio*, ed. and trans. Frank Barlow, Clarendon Press 1999.

Henry of Huntingdon, *The History of the English People,* ed. and trans. D. Greenway, Oxford Medieval Texts, Oxford University Press 1996.

King Harald's Saga, trans. Magnus Magnusson and Hermann Pálsson, Penguin, London 1966.

Orderic Vitalis, *The Ecclesiastical History*, books III and IV (vol. II), ed. and trans. Marjorie Chibnall, Oxford Medieval Texts, Oxford University Press 2002.

Orkneyinga Saga, the history of the Earls of Orkney, trans. Hermann Pálsson and Paul Edwards, Penguin, London 1978.

The Waltham Chronicle, ed. and trans. Leslie Watkiss and Marjorie Chibnall, Oxford Medieval Texts, Oxford University Press 1994.

William of Malmesbury, *The History of the English Kings*, i, ed. and trans. R. A. B. Mynors, R. M. Thomson and M. Winterbottom, Oxford Medieval Texts, Oxford University Press 1998.

William of Poitiers, *Gesta Guillelmi,* ed. and trans. R. H. C. Davis and Marjorie Chibnall, Oxford Medieval Texts, Oxford University Press 1998.

David M. Wilson, *The Bayeux Tapestry*, Thames and Hudson, London 2004.

SECONDARY SOURCES

Frank Barlow, *Edward the Confessor*, Eyre Methuen, London 1979.

Frank Barlow, *The English Church* 1000–1066, Longman, London 1979.

Frank Barlow, *The Godwins: the Rise and Fall of a Noble Dynasty*, Pearson Longman, London 2002.

David Bates, *William the Conqueror,* Tempus Publishing, Stroud 2004.

David Bates, *Normandy Before* 1066, Longmans, London 1982.

R. Howard Bloch, *A Needle in the Right Hand of God*, Random House, New York 2006.

Andrew Bridgeford, 1066: *The Hidden History of the Bayeux Tapestry*, Harper Perennial, London 2004.

F. W. Brooks, *The Battle of Stamford Bridge,* East Yorkshire Local
    History Society, York 1956.

R. Allen Brown, *The Normans and the Norman Conquest*, The Boydell
    Press, Woodbridge 1985.

A. H. Burne, *The Battlefields of England*, Penguin, London 2002.

James Campbell, *The Anglo-Saxon State*, Hambledon Press, London 2000.

James Campbell, *Essays in Anglo-Saxon History*, Hambledon Press,
    London 1986.

James Campbell, ed., *The Anglo-Saxons,* Penguin Books, London 1991.

Marjorie Chibnall, *The Debate on the Norman Conquest*, Manchester
    University Press 1999.

J. H. Clapham, 'The Horsing of the Danes', *English Historical Review*
    XXV (1910), 287–93.

Peter A. Clarke, *The English Nobility under Edward the Confessor*,
    Clarendon Press, Oxford 1994.

C. R. Dodwell, *Anglo-Saxon Art: A New Perspective*, Cornell University
    Press, Ithaca 1982.

David C. Douglas, *William the Conqueror*, University of California
    Press, Berkeley & Los Angeles 1964.

E. A. Freeman, *The History of the Norman Conquest of England, its
    Causes and Results*, Clarendon Press, Oxford 1867–79, 6 vols.
    (especially vols. 2 and 3).

Richard Gameson ed., *The Study of the Bayeux Tapestry*, The Boydell
    Press, Woodbridge 1997.

Paul Hill, *The Road to Hastings: The Politics of Power in Anglo-Saxon
    England*, Tempus Publishing, Stroud 2005.

C. Warren Hollister, *Anglo-Saxon Military Institutions on the Eve of the
    Norman Conquest*, Clarendon Press, Oxford 1962.

Eric John, 'Edward the Confessor and the Norman Succession', *English
    Historical Review*, 371 (1979), 241–67.

Charles Jones, *The Forgotten Battle of Fulford*, Tempus Publishing,
    Stroud 2007.

Sten Körner, *The Battle of Hastings, England and Europe 1035–1066*,
    Skånska Centraltryckeriet, Lund 1964.

Ryan Lavelle, *Æthelred II, King of the English 978–1016*, Tempus
    Publishing, Stroud 2002.

M. K. Lawson, *The Battle of Hastings 1066*, Tempus Publishing, Stroud
    2002.

M. K. Lawson, *Cnut, England's Viking King*, Tempus Publishing, Stroud 2004.

Charles H. Lemmon, *The Field of Hastings*, St Leonards-on-Sea 1970.

H. R. Loyn, *Anglo-Saxon England and the Norman Conquest,* Longmans Green, London 1966.

Frank McLynn, *1066: The Year of the Three Battles,* Pimlico, London 1999.

Emma Mason, *St Wulfstan of Worcester, c.*1005–1095, Oxford 1990.

Stephen Morillo, ed., *The Battle of Hastings, sources and interpretations,* The Boydell Press, Woodbridge 1999.

Catherine Morton, 'Pope Alexander II and the Norman Conquest', *Latomus*, XXXIV, Tournai 1975, 362–82.

Gale R. Owen-Crocker, *King Harold II and the Bayeux Tapestry*, The Boydell Press, Woodbridge 2005.

J. H. Round, *Feudal England*, Allen and Unwin, London 1964.

Pauline Stafford, *Queen Emma and Queen Edith,* Oxford 1997.

Sir Frank Stenton, *Anglo-Saxon England,* The Oxford History of England, Clarendon Press, Oxford 1962.

Sir Frank Stenton, ed., *The Bayeux Tapestry, a comprehensive survey*, Phaidon Press, London 1965.

Matthew Strickland ed., *Anglo-Norman Warfare: studies in late Anglo-Saxon and Anglo-Norman Warfare*, The Boydell Press, Woodbridge 1992.

Victoria Thompson, *Dying and Death in Later Anglo-Saxon England*, The Boydell Press, Woodbridge 2004.

Ian W. Walker, *Harold: The Last Anglo-Saxon King*, Sutton Publishing, Stroud 2004.

Dorothy Whitelock, *The Beginnings of English Society*, The Pelican History of England, London 1954.

Whitelock, Douglas, Lemmon and Barlow, *The Norman Conquest: Its Setting and Impact*, Eyre and Spottiswoode, London 1966.

Ann Williams, *The English and the Norman Conquest*, Boydell and Brewer, Woodbridge 1995.

Ann Williams, *Kingship and Government in Pre-Conquest England, c.500–1066*, Macmillan 1999.

David M. Wilson, *The Anglo-Saxons*, Penguin, London 1972.

INDEX

banner
  Fighting Man 70
  papal 140, 142–3
  Landwaster 150, 153, 156
Barlow, Frank 18, 80, 125, 126, 234
    n.vii, 237 n.lxvii
Bates, David 80–1, 236 n.xlv
Battle Abbey 142, 177–8
Battle Abbey Chronicle 174, 231
The Battle of Maldon 7–8, 58, 88, 215
Battles, full-scale 93–5
Baudri de Bourgeuil 181–2, 195, 230,
    231
Bayeux Tapestry 48, 50–1, 53, 229–31
  and armour 117–18, 178, 180
  and death of Harold 193–6, 230,
    231
  and English army 104, 116
  and Norman army 96, 174, 184
  and papal banner 142
  survival 67
  value as source 229–31, 232
  and weaponry 120
Bede, the Venerable 56–7, 76–7, 87
Benedict Biscop 77
Benedict VIII, Pope 12–13
Benedict X, Pope 237 n.lxxv
Beowulf 44, 69–70, 82–4, 118, 215
Bjorn Estrithson, Earl 27, 35–6
Blake, N. F. 215
blinding, as punishment 16–17, 194
Bloch, R. Howard 195–6
Boethius, The Consolation of
    Philosophy 93
Boniface of Mainz, St 76
Bosham, manor 50, 146–7, 196
Bretons, in Norman army 112, 132,
    183, 185–7, 189, 193
Brown, R. Allen 49, 110, 152,
    189–90, 193, 234 n.xv, 236 n.lix
Brunanburh, battle of (937) 95
burhs (fortified towns) 98–9, 136, 162
Burne, Col. A. H. 189

Byrhtnoth, ealdorman of Essex 7–8,
    58, 100, 109, 215
Byrhtwold 88

Caldbec Hill 2, 177–8, 180
Campbell, James 55, 60, 79–80, 82,
    234 n.xxi, 235 n.xxiii
Canterbury
  and Anglo-Saxon Chronicle 25, 219
  archbishopric 23, 137–8, 205–6
  and Bayeux Tapestry 53, 229
  Christ Church Abbey 53, 205, 225
  Codex Aureus 70
Caradoc ap Gruffydd 123
Carmen de Hastingæ Proelio 146,
    156–7, 159, 165, 171, 174–5,
    181–4, 191–2, 220–3
cavalry
  Anglo-Saxon 108–9, 120, 155–6,
    228
  Norman 96, 107, 108, 109–10,
    112–15, 118–19, 174, 178, 183,
    185–6, 193
Chanson de Roland 81, 184
chansons de geste 81, 214
Charlemagne 64, 75, 76
Charles the Simple, King of the
    Franks 6
Chibnall, Marjorie 111
Christ Church Abbey, Canterbury
    53, 205, 225
Christianity
  and learning 75–8
  as unifying factor 56–7, 66–7
Christina, daughter of Edward the
    Atheling 29
Church, English 11, 67–8, 136–41,
    205–7
churls 73, 100
Clapham, J. H. 109
Clark, Sir Kenneth 70

Index compiled by Meg Davies, Fellow of the Society of Indexers